2 CDs

Impact Listening 3

Kenton Harsch
Kate Wolfe-Quintero

Series Editor Michael Rost

Longman

Published by
Longman Asia ELT
2/F Cornwall House
Taikoo Place
979 King's Road
Quarry Bay
Hong Kong

fax: +852 2856 9578
e-mail: aelt@pearsoned.com.hk
www.longman.com

and Associated Companies throughout the world.

This book was developed for Longman Asia ELT by Lateral Communications Ltd., USA.

The publisher's policy is to use **paper manufactured from sustainable forests**

First published 2001
Reprinted 2002 (twice)

Produced by Pearson Education North Asia Limited, Hong Kong
GCC/06

PROJECT DIRECTOR, SERIES EDITOR: Michael Rost
PROJECT COORDINATOR: Keiko Kimura
PROJECT EDITORS: Terry Passero, Jenny Lorant,
              Anne McGannon Louis, Wendy Mazzoni
ART DIRECTOR: Lisa Ekstrom
DESIGN: Lisa Ekstrom, Keiko Kimura

PRODUCTION COORDINATOR: Eric Yau
ILLUSTRATIONS: Frank Ansley, Anna Veltfort, Gary Hallgren,
              Glenn Dudley, Jody Jobe
PHOTOGRAPHS: Mark Johann, Fox Images, PhotoDisc
RECORDING COORDINATOR: Ellen Schwartz
RECORDING ENGINEERS: Mary Ellen Perry, Glenn Davidson,
              David Joslyn
MUSIC: Music Bakery
WEBSITE COORDINATOR: John Cunha

IMPACT LISTENING 1
Student Book + Self Study CD ISBN 962 00 51335
Teacher's Manual ISBN 962 00 5136X
Classroom Cassettes Set ISBN 962 00 51394
Classroom CD Set ISBN 962 00 51424
Impact Listening 1 Test Pack ISBN 962 00 51459

IMPACT LISTENING 2
Student Book + Self Study CD ISBN 962 00 51343
Teacher's Manual ISBN 962 00 51378
Classroom Cassettes Set ISBN 962 00 51408
Classroom CD set ISBN 962 00 51432
Impact Listening 2 Test Pack ISBN 962 00 51467

IMPACT LISTENING 3
Student Book + Self Study CD ISBN 962 00 51351
Teacher's Manual ISBN 962 00 51386
Classroom Cassettes Set ISBN 962 00 51416
Classroom CD set ISBN 962 00 51440
Impact Listening 3 Test Pack ISBN 962 00 51475

Acknowledgements

The authors, editors and publishers would like to thank the lowing people who contributed so much to the developmer the *Impact Listening* series: First, we would like to thank the language teachers around the world who reviewed and pilo earlier versions of the textbooks:

Anthony Butera	Mike Laib	Elly Schottma
Jennifer Bixby	Elizabeth Lange	Maggie Sokoli
Karen Carrier	Ruth Larimer	Dianne Stark
Andrea Carvalho	Nyla Marnay	Judy Tanka
Christopher Decker	Michael Mew	John Thompso
John Doodigain	Akiko Mizoguchi	Joe Tomei
Bill Figoni	Yuko Nakajima	George Trusco
Tamotsu Fujita	William Newman	Carol Vaughn
Masayoshi Fukui	Yuko Ono	Susan Vik
Erik Gunderson	Allison Peck	Daniel Walsh
Naoya Hase	Arturo Pedroso	Kirk Wiltshire
Louise Haynes	Joyce Rossignol	Jerry Winn
Kyoko Kawagoe	Stephen Russell	Julie Winter
An-Ran Kim	Gauhar Sazanbaeva	Carolyn Wu
Masa Kobayashi		Yoko Yamazak

We would like to give special thanks to our colleagues at Pea Education who provided support and useful feedback during development of the series:

Joanne Dresner	Craig Zettle	Kate Lowe
Dugie Cameron	Nick Lutz	Karen Fraser
Karen Chiang	Allen Ascher	Chongdae Chu
Eleanor Barnes	Louisa Hellegers	Marion Coope
Mieko Otaka	Tom Sweeney	

Many people contributed to the shaping of the extracts fo *Impact Listening* and participated in the authentic recordir on which the final recordings were based, or took part in actual studio drafts and final recordings:

Hamed Abdel-Samad	Tom Lam	Carsten Roeve
Laura Jean Anderson	Marvin LeNoue	Cheryl Roorda
Selana Allen	Yan Liao	Jason Ramey
Cathy Harrison	Noriko Maegawa	Renata Schuh
Catherine Burriss	Terri Menacker	Sook Kyoung Stringer
Mark Brosamer	Christina Morrell	Ellen Schwartz
Melody Bryant	Patricia Mulholland	Eric Damon Sr
Peter Canavese	Purni Morell	Irma Spars
Feodor Chin	Rami Margron	Jerome Schwa
Martyn Clark	Tony Montemayor	Diane Tasca
Jennifer Dennison	Yuka Murakami	Paul Thompso
Tony Donnes	Carrie Olson	Rick Tabor
Lisa Fredericksen	Colleen Oakes	Stephanie Tay
Nathan Falstreau	Daniel Olmstead	Germaine Ven
David Gassner	Joy Osmanski	Edward Wallac
Justin Good	Amy Parker	Julie Wulferdi
Scott Grinthal	Bill Parry	Paul Wiesser
Katie Hemmeter	Heather Pierce	Cesar Zepeda
Paul Kent	Jackie Pels	
Aki Kurimoto	Michelle Powell	
	Rachel Peters	

Special thanks to the people who helped enhance the act ideas, particularly Eric Gunnarsen, Troy Miller and Randy "Jassman" Smith.

Introduction

The *Impact Listening* series is an innovative series of teaching materials to help learners develop listening and speaking ability. The series has three levels:

Impact Listening 1 (for beginners)
Impact Listening 2 (for high beginners)
Impact Listening 3 (for intermediate and advanced students)

There are five main principles on which the *Impact Listening* series is based:

1. Rich input   Learners need **rich input** in order to develop their language ability. The best input is **contextualized**, **based on authentic sources** and **interesting** for the learners. Input that is **slightly above the learners' proficiency level** provides a challenge to motivate learners. *Impact Listening* features extracts drawn from or based on authentic conversations and uses a wide variety of speakers to provide an abundance of interesting input.

2. Clear tasks   In order to develop their attention span, learners need guidance in **what to listen for**. Clear **tasks** guide the student in what to focus on and what to remember. **Task cycles** allow students to **listen to the same input more than once**, in order to practice controlling their attention. Each section in *Impact Listening* provides a transparent, structured task that is easy to use in the classroom.

3. Listening Strategies   In order to become more confident and relaxed, learners need to learn **how to listen**. By using successful listening strategies — **predicting**, **inferring**, **clarifying** and **responding** — learners will become more "fluent listeners." By **explicitly** including strategy instruction in the classroom, teachers encourage their students to learn more efficiently. These strategies are taught consistently throughout the *Impact Listening* series.

4. Language awareness   Listening provides an important opportunity for learners to experience language "in **real time**." By helping students **focus on form while listening**, teachers can help students acquire a deeper understanding of grammar and vocabulary. Each unit in *Impact Listening* provides a Language Awareness activity to maximize learning from listening.

5. Self-expression   The central purpose of listening is application — using the ideas in the conversation and formulating some kind of response. By incorporating **self-expression** steps with listening activities, students increase their overall oral language ability. *Impact Listening* features a variety of short speaking activities as well as an extended Interaction Link in each unit to build conversational skills alongside listening skills.

The unit design of *Impact Listening* allows for clear implementation of these principles. Each unit has four main sections: **Vocabulary Task, Listening Task, Real World Listening** and **Language Awareness**, plus an **Interaction Link** and a **Self-Study Page** in the Appendix. All activities are designed to be easy to use in any classroom setting.

Unit Components

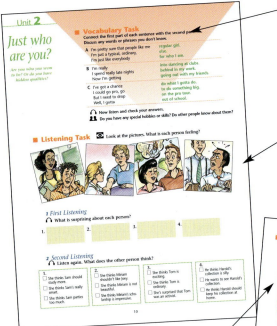

Vocabulary Task

This section introduces new words and phrases, and previews the unit topics. By including a warm-up speaking task, the Vocabulary Task gets all students involved at the outset of the lesson.

Listening Task

The Listening Task is a set of two linked tasks based on four short extracts. The First Listening task focuses on understanding the gist of the input, while the Second Listening task focuses on detail and interpretation. This section employs illustrations or photographs to help students predict the content. This section also includes a short follow-up speaking activity.

Real World Listening

Based on unscripted recordings, this section provides a lively variety of extracts and engaging tasks. The Real World Listening section teaches listening strategies and helps students predict, infer and respond to the ideas in the extract.

Language Awareness

Based on language points in the unit listening extracts, this section helps students analyze key points of grammar, vocabulary and phonology that affect listening.

Interaction Link

This Interaction Link is a lively speaking activity, role play or game directly related to the unit topics and functions.

Self-Study Page

For use with the Self-Study CD, the Self-Study Page provides new tasks for the Real World Listening extract, to allow students to review at home. The Self-Study CD also contains the Language Awareness section, for at-home review.

Teacher's Manual

Teachers are encouraged to utilize the *Impact Listening* Teacher's Manual. This manual contains teaching procedures, insightful language and culture notes, full scripts, answer keys, expansion activities and review tests.

Website

Teachers and students are welcome to use the *Impact* series website additional ideas and resources.

<www.impactseries.com/listening

To the Student

Impact Listening will help you use listening strategies. Listening strategies are ways of thinking actively as you listen. Here are the main strategies you will practice in this course:

Predict

Predicting helps you become an active listener. (It doesn't matter if your prediction is right!)
Before you listen, think about the ideas. Look at illustrations and photographs. Look over the vocabulary words. Try to guess what will happen. Try to predict what the speakers will say.

Ask

Thinking of questions — and asking questions — will help you become a more active listener.
Good listeners ask questions. *While you listen*, think of questions you can ask to help you understand more. Try to make *specific* questions. *After you listen*, ask your teacher or other students about things you don't understand.

Guess

Guessing (making inferences) can make you a more successful listener.
When we listen, the information is often incomplete or unclear. There are words and ideas we don't understand fully. And there are ideas that the speaker doesn't express clearly.) In order to listen, we have to guess. Make your best guess at the parts you don't understand.

Respond

Responding makes you a more interactive listener.
While you listen, pay attention to the speaker. *After you listen*, respond to the ideas. Think about the content: What do you think?

Focus

Focusing on the key ideas helps you to concentrate.
Before you listen, look at the listening task or questions. *While you listen*, focus on the key words. You don't have to understand every word. Use the words you understand. Try to form a main idea. If there are some words you don't understand, that's OK. Keep listening.

Review

Reviewing helps you develop your memory.
After you listen, think about the meaning of what the speakers have said. Try to say the meaning *in your own words*.

Contents

er	Theme	Title	Vocabulary Task	Listening Task	Real World Listening	Language Awareness	Interaction Link
	Travel pages 28 - 29	*Getting there is half the fun*	Things that happen while traveling, feelings about travel experiences	Narrating events from travels	A traveler tells about an experience in Thailand	Definite and indefinite noun phrases	Swapping Travel Stories: Telling and re-telling stories
	Business pages 30 - 31	*Real money*	Investments, what happens when you invest, attitudes toward investing	Talking about the pros and cons of different investments	An infomercial for a money-making video	Countable and non-countable nouns	You May Already Have Won! Discussing what to do with a huge amount of money
	Schedules pages 32 - 33	*Never enough free time!*	Things you like to do in your free time, obligations, feelings about free time	Talking about things one has to do and things one likes to do in one's free time	Two co-workers talk about commuting and free time	Simple and phrasal modals	Not Enough Money or Not Enough Time: Discussing how to spend limited free time
	Weather pages 34 - 35	*Disaster!*	Disasters, the effects of disasters, and how people respond to them	Describing disasters and narrating the events around disasters	A woman describes her experience in an earthquake	Present perfect and present continuous tenses	Emergency Aid: Discussing what aid items to send to a disaster area
	Entertainment pages 36 - 37	*Who needs advice?*	Types of personal problems, how to give advice	Describing personal problems, giving advice	A woman calls in to a radio talk show	Verbs and phrasal verbs followed by prepositions	Advice Column: Discussing what advice to give someone with a problem
	Home pages 38 - 39	*Fixing up the place*	Talking about your living space and things you could buy or do to fix it up	Suggesting ways to fix up the place, agreeing or disagreeing	Two married college students talk about decorating their apartment	Use of gerunds vs. bare verbs when giving opinions and suggestions	Fixing Up the Place: Discussing how to decorate or remodel an apartment
	Health pages 40 - 41	*Losing someone*	Talking about a loved one who has passed away, expressing grief and condolences	Giving condolences, when someone loses a loved one	An elderly man remembers his wife who passed away	*Yes-no* and *wh-* questions with and without inversion	Who Would You Bring Back? Discussing who from history you would like to bring back to life
	Shopping pages 42 - 43	*How can I help you?*	Things service people and salespeople say to customers	Sales and service people offering to help customers, making suggestions	A man has trouble returning a shirt	Noun clauses as objects	And the Service is Great! Discussing the qualities of great service for different businesses
	Food pages 44 - 45	*Putting food on the table*	Preparing to cook, types of food and cooking, feelings about cooking	Talking about different options for preparing or having a meal	Two college roommates talk about preparing meals	Interrogative clauses as subjects and objects	Cook or Eat Out? Talking about what food or restaurant would be best in different situations
	News pages 46 - 47	*Breaking news*	Descriptions of news, how news is presented, talking about the news informally	Newscasters narrating events in the news	Two college students talk about international affairs	Active and passive verbs	Repercussions: Discussing the probability and the after-effects of different events

Old friends, different choices

Different people make different choices in their lives. What will you choose in the future?

■ Vocabulary Task

Connect the first part of each sentence with the second part. Discuss any words or phrases you don't know.

A
It's been 10 years since I	see the world.
I was able to travel and	being a housewife!
And I never got stuck	saw you last.

B
Things are going	9 to 5 at a neighborhood store.
I finally settled	great for me these days.
Now I work	down and got a real job.

C
Life has sure treated	through school.
I put myself	me well.
I was able to work	my own business.
And then I started	my way up in a company.

🎧 Now listen and check your answers.

👥 Which of these life choices appeal to you? Have you ever run into some one after not seeing them for a long time? What did you talk about?

■ Listening Task 👁 Look at the pictures. Where are these people meeting?

1 First Listening
🎧 What did each person do with their life?

1. 2. 3. 4.

2 Second Listening
🎧 Listen again. How do they feel about their decisions?

1.
☐ He disliked living abroad.
☐ He missed his home.

2.
☐ She feels she's still young enough to be a model.
☐ She hopes her daughter will become a model.

3.
☐ He loves his family.
☐ He wants a better job.

4.
☐ She's proud of job.
☐ She wishes she gone to college

Real World Listening

1 Predict

Karen and Sharon are meeting for the first time after many years. **What do you think they will talk about?**

☐ travel   ☐ old boyfriends

☐ family   ☐ career

☐ other things _____

🎧 **Now listen and check your prediction.**

2 Get the main ideas

Read each statement. Write T for *True* or F for *False*.

____ Sharon and Karen haven't seen each other for 30 years.

____ Sharon planned to get married to Jim after high school.

____ Sharon started her own advertising agency.

____ Sharon majored in art in college.

____ Karen didn't want to get stuck being a housewife.

____ Karen had one child.

____ Karen traveled around Europe for a year.

____ Karen went to medical school.

3 Respond to the ideas

1. Do you think either Sharon or Karen has any regrets about the choices they have made?

2. Tell about a major choice you have made in your life and why you chose it. If you had it to do again, would you make the same choice? Why or why not?

Language Awareness: Past and future hopes

🎧 **Listen and write the missing words.**

A: Hey, Julie, how are you? I haven't seen you in a long time!

B: Yeah, Bill, the last time I saw you, you __*were going to*__ become a TV news anchor. Did that happen?

A: Well, not really. I _____ in broadcasting in college, and I _____ become famous and travel all around the world. I _____ report on important world events. But instead, I just _____ a local news reporter.

B: That sounds like a good job.

A: Yeah, it is, but I _____ to travel. That's what I really _____ I could do. So I _____ for an international news position.

B: Maybe it's not too late!

Put each phrase where it belongs.

PAST HOPES	PAST EVENTS	FUTURE HOPES
• *were going to*	• *majored*	• *want*
•	•	•
•	•	•

👥 What is the difference between *I was going to* and *I am going to*?

> **INTERACTION LINK**
> *Life Choices*
>
> ➡ *page 49*

Just who are you?

Are you who you seem to be? Or do you have hidden qualities?

■ **Vocabulary Task**

Connect the first part of each sentence with the second part.
Discuss any words or phrases you don't know.

A I'm pretty sure that people like me	regular girl.
I'm just a typical, ordinary,	else.
I'm just like everybody	for who I am.

B I'm really	into dancing at clubs.
I spend really late nights	behind in my work.
Now I'm getting	going out with my friends.

C I've got a chance	do what I gotta do.
I could go pro, go	to do something big.
But I need to drop	on the pro tour.
Well, I gotta	out of school.

🎧 **Now listen and check your answers.**

👥 **Do you have any special hobbies or skills? Do other people know about t**

■ **Listening Task**   👁 Look at the pictures. What is each person feeling?

1 First Listening

🎧 What is surprising about each person?

1.   2.   3.   4.

2 Second Listening

🎧 Listen again. What does the other person think?

1.
- [ ] She thinks Sam should study more.
- [ ] She thinks Sam's really smart.
- [ ] She thinks Sam parties too much.

2.
- [ ] She thinks Miriam shouldn't like Joey.
- [ ] She thinks Miriam is not beautiful.
- [ ] She thinks Miriam's scholarship is impressive.

3.
- [ ] She thinks Tom is exciting.
- [ ] She thinks Tom is ordinary.
- [ ] She's surprised that Tom was an activist.

4.
- [ ] He thinks Harold's collection is silly.
- [ ] He wants to see H collection.
- [ ] He thinks Harold s keep his collection home.

Real World Listening

1 *Predict*

Cesar and TJ are talking about a contest that TJ won.
Look at the pictures of TJ. **What do you think he is good at?**

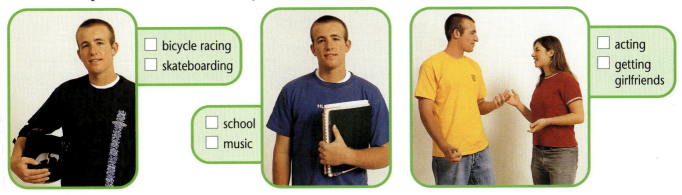

- ☐ bicycle racing
- ☐ skateboarding
- ☐ school
- ☐ music
- ☐ acting
- ☐ getting girlfriends

 Now listen and check your prediction.

2 *Get the main ideas*

Read each statement. Write **T** for *True*, **F** for *False*, or **X** for *Don't Know*.

___ TJ got second place in the pro skateboarding contest last weekend.

___ TJ is going to do a TV commercial.

___ Cesar thinks TJ will forget his friends after he becomes famous.

___ TJ feels like a regular guy.

___ TJ has a girlfriend.

___ TJ's parents don't want him to drop out of school.

___ TJ doesn't want to drop out of school.

___ Cesar wants TJ to drop out of school.

3 *Respond to the ideas*

1. Do you think TJ will forget his friends as he gets more famous? Why or why not?
2. Would you rather be a regular person or someone who is famous? Is it possible to be both?

Language Awareness: Idioms

Listen and write the missing words.

A: Hey, what's Sally ___*up to*___ these days?

B: Didn't you hear? She hit _____ .

A: What do you mean?

B: She got a part on a daytime TV soap opera.

A: No kidding. I knew she was _____ acting, but I never thought she'd _____ .

B: Yeah, she decided to _____ , so she moved to L.A.

A: Wow, she's _____ , isn't she? She must be getting _____ .

B: Yep. Boy, has she _____ .

Put each phrase where it belongs.

idioms with *be*	idioms with *it*	idioms that are nouns
• is ___*up to*___ something	• *make it big*	• *the big time*
• was _____ something	•	•
	•	•

What verb is used with each noun idiom?

INTERACTION LINK
Who Are You Really?
➡ *page 50*

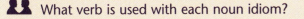

11

Unit 3

Living with people

Who do you live with?
*Or do you live
by yourself?*

■ Vocabulary Task

Connect the first part of each sentence with the second part.
Discuss any words or phrases you don't know.

A Dorm life has — some major negatives.
The other students keep — me up all night.
And my roommate doesn't give — me any space.

B My new roommate doesn't drive — me crazy.
She never leaves — her food or clothes all over the place.
She never takes — my things without asking.

C My dad's rules — are way too strict.
He won't let me — use the phone for more than 10 minut[es]
And I have to — be back by a 9 p.m. curfew.
I know it's because he's — concerned about me.

🎧 Now listen and check your answers.

👥 Do you live with a roommate or your family? What are those people like?

■ Listening Task 👁 Look at the pictures. What problems do you think these people [have?]

1 First Listening
🎧 What problems are they talking about?

1. _____   2. _____   3. _____   4. _____

2 Second Listening
🎧 Listen again. Check the details that the speakers mention.

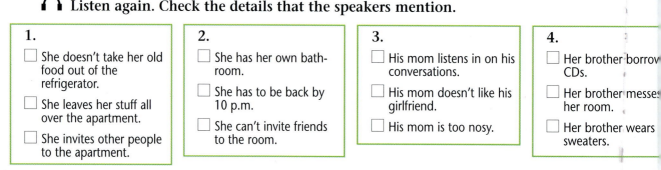

1.	2.	3.	4.
☐ She doesn't take her old food out of the refrigerator.	☐ She has her own bathroom.	☐ His mom listens in on his conversations.	☐ Her brother borrow[s] CDs.
☐ She leaves her stuff all over the apartment.	☐ She has to be back by 10 p.m.	☐ His mom doesn't like his girlfriend.	☐ Her brother messe[s] her room.
☐ She invites other people to the apartment.	☐ She can't invite friends to the room.	☐ His mom is too nosy.	☐ Her brother wears [her] sweaters.

Real World Listening

1 Predict

Look at the picture.
Kara lives with the Johnsons, an elderly couple.
What problems do you think she might have?

☐ They expect her to take care of them.
☐ They make her come home early.
☐ They don't respect her privacy.
☐ They give her terrible food.
☐ Something else? _____

🎧 Now listen and check your prediction.

2 Get the main ideas

Read each statement. Write ✔ for *"it bothers Kara,"*
or ? for *"no information."*

☐ The rent is too high.
☐ Mrs. Johnson visits Kara too often.
☐ Mrs. Johnson's soup is terrible.
☐ Mrs. Johnson watches her while she eats.
☐ Mr. and Mrs. Johnson make too much noise.
☐ Mrs. Johnson wants to know where she is going.
☐ Mr. Johnson tries to hug and kiss her all the time.

3 Respond to the ideas

1. What do you think Kara should do?
2. Have you ever lived with a homestay family or some roommates? What were the good and bad things about living with them?

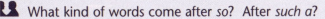

Language Awareness: *So* and *such a*

🎧 **Listen and write the missing words.**

A: Hey, sis! You're so __*messy*__ — you drive me crazy! I wish you wouldn't leave your stuff all over the place. Why don't you keep your clothes out of the bathroom once in a while — it's so _____ to find them laying around in there all the time. You're such a _____ .

B: Yeah, well, if you weren't such a _____ , I wouldn't do that. You're so _____ , and so _____ , too. You don't give me my phone messages, and you never wash your dirty dishes. You're such a _____ . I don't see how anyone can stand to live with you.

A: You see? Just listen to you. You're such a _____ .

Put each phrase where it belongs.

phrases that come after *so*	phrases that come after *such a*
• messy	• messy person
•	•
•	•
•	•

👥 What kind of words come after *so*? After *such a*?

INTERACTION LINK
Complain About...

➡ *page 51*

13

Unit **4**

High fashion, low budget

Are you into high fashion? Or are you on a tight budget?

■ Vocabulary Task

Connect the first part of each sentence with the second part.
Discuss any words or phrases you don't know.

A	I'm trying to	credit cards are for.
	But this sweater may	watch my spending.
	Oh, well, that's what	never be this cheap again!

B	If only I could	afford this killer dress.
	I guess I'll have to wait until	to save up enough money.
	In the meantime, I'll try	it's on sale.

C	This style is really	got to have one.
	It's the	*in* this year.
	I know I'm just paying	latest thing.
	But it's so me. I've just	for the designer's name.

Now listen and check your answers.

Which of these reasons for buying something are important to you
Do you have enough money to get the things that you want?

■ Listening Task Look at the pictures. What are they planning to buy?

1 First Listening

Describe each item.

1. 2. 3. 4.

2 Second Listening

Listen again. Why do they want to buy it?

1. 2. 3. 4.

14

Real World Listening

1 *Predict*

Susie just arrived in New York
to visit her cousin Rachel.
**Look at the pictures of Susie
and Rachel.
Are they different?
Are they alike?
How?**

🎧 Now listen and check your prediction.

Susie

Rachel

2 *Get the main ideas*

1. Why did Susie come to visit?
2. What's on Susie's shopping list?
3. Is Susie going to buy something for Rachel?
4. What does Susie want from Rachel?

3 *Respond to the ideas*

1. Rachel says, "I don't want anyone to buy me something that I can't afford myself." Is that
   how you feel?
2. Are you a "fashionable" person or a "jeans and T-shirt" person?

Language Awareness: Types of phrases

🎧 **Listen and write the missing words.**

A: What am I __*going to*__ do? It's so depressing.

B: What's _____ ?

A: I don't have enough money. I'm really _____ designer clothes, but I just can't afford them.

B: You and I are _____ . I would never buy designer clothes, 'cause I'm _____ to watch my spending.

A: Well, I'm _____ a student budget, too. But there's this $500 dress I really want!

B: It's your _____ ! But you're _____ . You need that money to live on.

A: I know. I just can't help it.

Put each phrase where it belongs.

nouns	prepositions	verbs	adjectives
• the problem	• into	• going to	• really different
•	•	•	•

👥 Each of these types of phrases comes after the same verb.
What is that verb?

INTERACTION LINK
Design a Wardrobe

➡ *page 52*

15

So many kinds of English

People use English differently around the world. Different accents, different vocabulary, sometimes even different grammar. What standard should we use?

■ **Vocabulary Task**

Connect the first part of each sentence with the second part.
Discuss any words or phrases you don't know.

A		
Sometimes I have trouble	use a lot of slang.	
That's because native speakers	could speak English more fluen	
I wish I	understanding native speakers	

B		
I want a teacher who is	spoke the same way.	
And I think everyone should learn	a native speaker of English.	
It would make communication easier if we all	standard American English.	

C		
English is the language	from all over the place.	
People who speak English come	to how someone else speaks.	
Everyone who speaks English has an accent	of international communicatio of some kind.	
Sometimes you have to get used		

∩ Listen and check your answers.

👥 Which of these ideas do you agree with? What different kinds of E have you heard? Where did you hear them?

■ **Listening Task** 👁 Look at the pictures. What do these people need English fo

1 *First Listening*
∩ What problem is the person talking about?

1.   2.   3.   4.

2 *Second Listening*
∩ Listen again. How does the listener respond?

1.   2.   3.   4.

Real World Listening

1 Predict

Look at the pictures.

Irma has a degree in travel management. She's applying for a job at a travel agency. **What job do you think she's applying for?**

☐ tour guide
☐ customer service representative
☐ department manager
☐ secretary
☐ another position _____

🎧 **Now listen and check your prediction.**

2 Get the main ideas

🎧 **Listen again. Answer these questions.**
1. Who do you think Irma is talking to?
2. What job did she get?
3. What qualifications does she have?
4. Why didn't she get the job she wanted?
5. What is she going to do next?

3 Respond to the ideas

1. What do you think Irma should do?
2. Are there any jobs that can be done only by native speakers of English? What jobs? Why?

Language Awareness: Verbs and participles

🎧 **Listen and write the missing words.**

It's great because lately, I don't ___*have*___ any trouble _____ understood when I use English. I _____ to this country _____ nothing, but I worked hard to learn English. Then I went to college and got a degree in computer science. Now I _____ a job _____ programs for a computer company. I _____ experience _____ that in college, and I know that my ability with English is going to help me get a good job.

Put each phrase in the correct column.

main verbs	participles
have	• *being*
	•
	•
	•

👤 What kind of words come between each verb and participle?

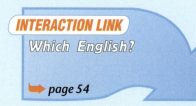

INTERACTION LINK

Which English?

➡ *page 54*

Unit **6**

Choosing a mate

When people choose their partners for life, what kind of people do they look for?

■ Vocabulary Task

Connect the first part of each sentence with the second part.
Discuss any words or phrases you don't know.

A	I know he	I can really trust.
	He's	is the one.
	He is someone	ready for a lifetime commitment.

B	I had doubts at first about	the relationship.
	He was divorced once already but	like the same things.
	Then I discovered that we	wanted to try again.

C	She swept me away	of humor.
	She has a great sense	my type.
	She's easy to talk to and fun	with her personality.
	And she's	to be with.

🎧 Now listen and check your answers.

👥 How much do money, education, job, personality, family, or previous marriage matter to you when you choose a partner?

■ Listening Task 👁 Look at the four people. What do you think they are like?

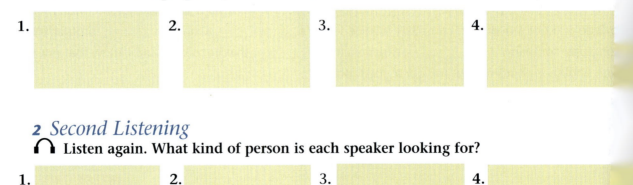

1   **2**   **3**   **4**

1 First Listening
🎧 What do these people say about themselves?

1.   2.   3.   4.

2 Second Listening
🎧 Listen again. What kind of person is each speaker looking for?

1.   2.   3.   4.

Real World Listening

1 Predict

Amy is talking about her fiancé Luis.
What do you think she likes about him?

☐ He's wealthy

☐ He's an athlete

☐ He's handsome

☐ He's educated

☐ He dresses very well

☐ He's romantic

☐ He's so funny

🎧 **Now listen and check your prediction.**

2 Get the main ideas

Which of these statements describe Luis?

☐ He's handsome.
☐ He looks like a Greek statue.
☐ He's got big hands.
☐ His clothes are fashionable.

☐ He's tall.
☐ He's sweet and funny.
☐ He's easy to be with.
☐ He's so romantic.

3 Respond to the ideas

1. Is Luis Amy's type? Why or why not?
2. What things are important to you when you first meet someone? What things do you want in a person you want to live with forever? Are they the same? Why or why not?

Language Awareness: Relative clauses

🎧 **Listen and write the missing words.**

You know, I don't think this relationship is going to work out. I want someone __who likes__ watching TV, but she wants someone who likes reading novels. I want someone _____ dancing every night, but she wants someone _____ to museums with. I want someone _____ a lot of money, but she wants someone _____ about things like that. And here's the biggest problem: I want someone _____ to have fun, but she wants someone _____. I don't think I'm the right guy.

Put each phrase where it belongs.

relative clauses with *who*
* who likes
*
*

relative clauses without *who*
* she can go
*
*

Can the *who* be deleted in the first group of relative clauses? Why or why not?

INTERACTION LINK
Matchmakers

➡ *page 55*

One big happy family

Do you have a large family, or a small one? Are there any interesting characters in your family?

■ Vocabulary Task

Connect the first part of each sentence with the second part. Discuss any words or phrases you don't know.

A My husband got
My son is
He's my son

from my first marriage.
transferred across the country.
feeling kind of bummed out.

B I never get to say
I got stuck with
It's like

what goes on in my own house.
taking care of the twin brats wh
    Mom works late.
a zoo around here.

C My husband can't
His weight is
My son and daughter-in-law had to
We have

move back home to help out.
no one else we can turn to.
causing him trouble with his leg
get around by himself anymore

🎧 Now listen and check your answers.

👥 What kinds of difficult situations has your family faced? How did you help out?

■ Listening Task 👁 Look at the pictures. What are the relationships between the pe

1 First Listening

🎧 Listen to each speaker. Put the speaker's name in the family tree.

1. Fred
2. Lyle
3. Lily
4. Eddie

Jeanne

Simon   Gloria   Sharc

Kristy   Shawna

Marty

2 Second Listening

🎧 Listen again. What does each speaker say about Gloria?

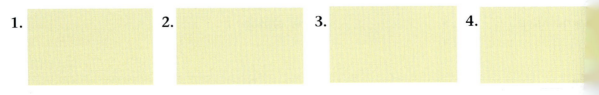

1.   2.   3.   4.

Real World Listening

1 Predict

Marty and Eddie are talking about their family. **What do you think they are worrying about?**

☐ Their mother nags them too much.

☐ They are being moved out of their room.

☐ Their grandmother is sick.

☐ They don't have enough time with their parents.

☐ Something else?
_____

 Now listen and check your prediction.

2 Get the main ideas

Read each statement. Write T for _True_ or F for _False_

___ Kristy and Shawna are moving in with Gloria's family.

___ Simon got transferred to Louisiana.

___ Lily, Simon's wife, doesn't have time to take care of her children.

___ Marty and Eddie have to sleep in the living room.

___ Gloria wants to solve everyone's problems.

___ Gloria asked Marty what he wants.

___ Grandma is feeling a lot better now.

___ Eddie is going to spend more time with Marty.

3 Respond to the ideas

1. Do you think this is a happy family? Why or why not?
2. Are there blended families or multi-generation families in your culture? What are the advantages and disadvantages?

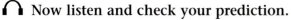

Language Awareness: Connectors

🎧 **Listen and write the missing words.**

Hi, I'm Gloria. ___When___ my parents asked me to move back home, I felt I had to, _____ my mom was having so much trouble. I didn't know if Lyle would be willing, _____ he was really good about it.

_____ we moved in, Marty and Eddie adjusted really well to living here, _____ they have their own room. _____ now, my nieces are coming to live with us _____ things are going to get more difficult. _____ they come, I need to get Marty and Eddie ready for the changes.

Put each phrase where it belongs.

connectors showing _time_	connectors showing _reason_	connectors showing _contrast_
• when	• because	• but
•	•	
•		

INTERACTION LINK

Family Lies

👥 **Which sentences have more than one connector?**
For each, which two parts are most closely connected?

➡ *page 56*

In a new culture

Have you ever lived in a different culture, or are you living in a different culture now? Was it easy or hard to get used to?

■ Vocabulary Task

Connect the first part of each sentence with the second part. Discuss any words or phrases you don't know.

A I really like
I can't get over
I would like

to live out my life here.
the way it is here, how safe it is.
how friendly and helpful people are

B I've gotten used
I used to try
But now I never think

to figure out why they do things a certain way.
twice about it.
to it here.

C Sometimes foreigners are
They shouldn't try to
They should just
Otherwise, they're not going to

last long.
relax and go with the flow.
too inflexible.
convert us to their way of doing th

🎧 Now listen and check your answers.

👥 Have you ever traveled to another country? What things did you like? What things bugged you?

■ Listening Task 👁 Look at the pictures. What cultural topic are they talking abou

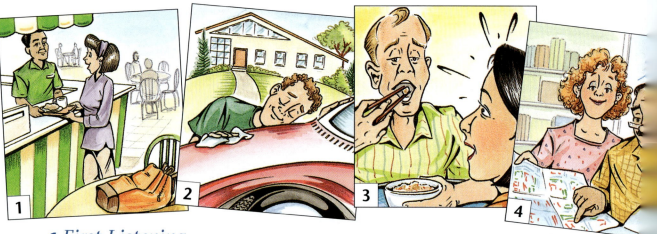

1 First Listening
🎧 Are they talking about something they like or dislike about the culture?

1. ☐ like ☐ dislike   2. ☐ like ☐ dislike   3. ☐ like ☐ dislike   4. ☐ like ☐ dis

2 Second Listening
🎧 Listen again. What did they say about the culture?

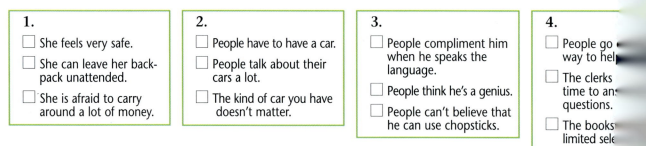

1.
☐ She feels very safe.
☐ She can leave her back-pack unattended.
☐ She is afraid to carry around a lot of money.

2.
☐ People have to have a car.
☐ People talk about their cars a lot.
☐ The kind of car you have doesn't matter.

3.
☐ People compliment him when he speaks the language.
☐ People think he's a genius.
☐ People can't believe that he can use chopsticks.

4.
☐ People go way to hel
☐ The clerks time to an questions.
☐ The books limited sele

eal World Listening

Predict

ve and Trish are colleagues who teach glish in Japan. Steve is telling Trish out two cultural differences. **What do** **1 think he is talking about?**

☐ the food
☐ store clerks
☐ crowds
☐ transportation
☐ eating habits
☐ language
☐ social rules

Now listen and check your prediction.

Get the main ideas

10 said this? **Write S for *Steve*, T for *Trish*, or X for *neither*.**

__ I don't like all of the packaging.
__ That's the way it is here.
__ They are too flexible here.
__ You have to just relax and go with the flow.
__ You're not going to last long.
__ The whole system is a waste of my time.
__ The clerks are really rude here.
__ I like the traditions.

Respond to the ideas

Who do you agree with more, Steve or Trish?

Some people say, "When in Rome, do as the Romans do." Others say it's important to keep your own cultural identity. What do you think?

anguage Awareness: Specific and general nouns

Listen and write the missing words.

have found that when I visit Japan, people give me __*gifts*__ all the time. Once I was on the bullet ain and _____ and a woman sitting next to me shared part of their meal with me, and then we lked for a long time. Then _____ gave me _____ from his hometown. It was a beautiful, andpainted picture of a bird. I accepted _____ from him but I was embarrassed, because I didn't ave _____ for him. In this kind of situation, I'd like to be able to give _____ in return, so ow I take _____ with me whenever I travel.

It each phrase where it belongs.

buns that refer to a real, existing thing
• *a man*   •

nouns that refer to a type, no particular one
• *gifts*   •
                    •

INTERACTION LINK
What's Bugging You?
➡ *page 57*

Why doesn't the speaker use the definite article *the* when ft or gifts are mentioned more than once?

23

High-tech gadgets

Do you always buy the latest high-tech equipment? Or do you know someone who does? Remember, there is always a new model coming out!

■ Vocabulary Task

Connect the first part of each sentence with the second part.
Discuss any words or phrases you don't know.

A The solar car   on the cutting edge of technology.
This car is right   in your neighborhood to have one.
Be the first   of the future is here today.

B Introducing a revolutionary   and order yours today.
It's incredibly convenient   and will make your life so easy.
Come visit our website   new product — the personal cash ma

C The homework machine is   extremely user friendly.
It does all the work for you   a college student's dream!
This new model is   expensive to upgrade.
And it's not too   automatically.

🎧 Now listen and check your answers.

👥 Which of these products would you be interested in having? Do y
think any of them are possible in the future? Why or why not?

■ Listening Task 👁 Look at the pictures. What do you think these inventions can

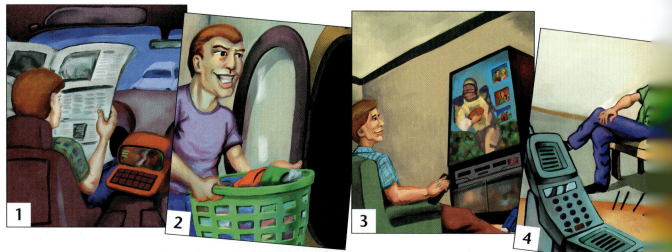

1   **2**   **3**   **4**

1 First Listening
🎧 What does each product do?

1.   2.   3.   4.

2 Second Listening
🎧 Listen again. Why are these inventions attractive?

1.   2.   3.   4.

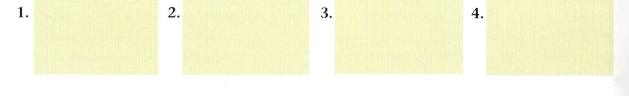

Real World Listening

1 Predict

What are some things that high-tech computers can do?

- ☐ [blank]
- ☐ [blank]
- ☐ [blank]
- ☐ [blank]
- ☐ [blank]

🎧 Now listen and check the things that Andy's new computer system can do.

2 Get the main ideas

What do Bob and Andy mean by these lines?

1. Bob says, "Is that another new computer?"
2. Andy says, "Speaking of computers, how's yours?"
3. Andy says, "Are you sure it meets all your needs?"
4. Bob says, "I doubt I'll need a new one anytime soon."
5. Andy says, "There's always a new model coming out."
6. Andy says, "You'll get left behind."

3 Respond to the ideas

1. Andy speaks about several new features of his computer. Which of these are attractive to you?
2. How important is it for you to keep up with technology? Do you worry about being left behind?

Language Awareness: Conditionals with *if* and *while*

🎧 **Listen and write the missing words.**

Steve doesn't have $3,000. But if he __*did have*__ the money, he would _____ the CellMate zoom phone. If he _____ a CellMate, he would never have to waste time again. While he _____ a shower, he could say a friend's name and the phone would _____ for him. He could talk while he _____ his hair, without even holding the phone. If he _____ in class, his girlfriend could call him and talk to him on the earphone. While he _____ to her, he could pretend to be listening to the teacher. The teacher would never know!

Put each phrase in the correct column.

if-clause verbs	while-clause verbs	would-clause verbs
• *did have*	• *was taking*	• *buy*
•	•	•
•	•	

What tense are the *if*-clause and *while*-clause verbs?
What time do they refer to?

INTERACTION LINK

Future Toys

➡ *page 58*

Unit **10**

Bad habits

Do you have any bad habits? Have you quit any bad habits that you used to have? How did you quit?

■ Vocabulary Task

Connect the first part of each sentence with the second part. Discuss any words or phrases you don't know.

A Whenever he's stressed   two or three packs a day to
    He likes to smoke   the habit.
    He's really got to kick   out, he has a few cigarettes

B He needs   for a few years now.
    He's been   professional help.
    He's been addicted   gambling way too much.

C She acts too   childish she looks.
    She just can't stop   with the ends of her hair.
    And she's always playing   nervous around me.
    The more she does it, the more   biting her fingernails.

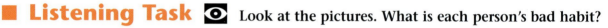 Now listen and check your answers.

What kinds of bad habits bother you? What bad habits do you

■ Listening Task   Look at the pictures. What is each person's bad habit?

| 1 | 2 | 3 | 4 |

1 First Listening
Write two details about each habit.

1. •
  •

2. •
  •

3. •
  •

4. •
  •

2 Second Listening
Listen again. What advice is given to the speaker?

1. *You've...*

2. *You'd better...*

3. *He needs...*

4. *Don't let...*

Real World Listening

1 Predict

Julie is visiting her doctor.
**Which of these habits do
you think her doctor will
talk to her about?**

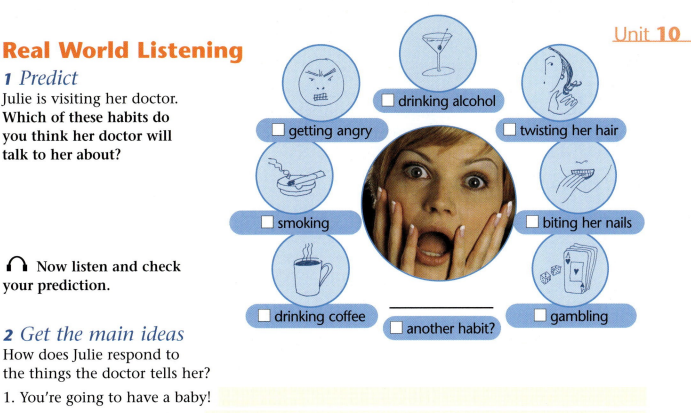

☐ drinking alcohol

☐ getting angry

☐ twisting her hair

☐ smoking

☐ biting her nails

🎧 Now listen and check
your prediction.

☐ drinking coffee

_____
☐ another habit?

☐ gambling

2 Get the main ideas

How does Julie respond to
the things the doctor tells her?

1. You're going to have a baby!

2. You need to stop smoking.

3. You can't drink while you're pregnant.

4. Coffee.

5. It's important to get regular exercise.

3 Respond to the ideas

1. Which of the doctor's suggestions do you think is most important for Julie to do?
2. Do you know anyone who quit smoking or drinking? How did they do it?

Language Awareness: Infinitives and gerunds

🎧 **Listen and write the missing words.**

A: I want to _*quit*_____ eating so much junk food, but I don't know how.

B: Do you _____ eating junk food?

A: Not really, but I _____ to eat, and I don't _____ to cook, so there you go. It's easy. Besides,
I _____ clothes shopping almost every day, so I buy my food out.

B: Well, that's your problem! You have to _____ going shopping!

A: Yeah, maybe you're right. I _____ looking for new clothes because I'm getting fat around the middle. But I guess I'm getting fat because I eat junk food. So maybe I can _____ to quit both of them
at the same time.

Put each phrase in the correct column.

verbs followed by infinitives	verbs followed by gerunds	
need	• _quit_	•
•	•	
•		

👥 Which of these verbs can occur with both gerunds and
finitives? Does the meaning change?

INTERACTION LINK

Kick the Habit

➡ *page 59*

Getting there is half the fun

What kinds of things have happened to you while you were traveling?

■ Vocabulary Task

Connect the first part of each sentence with the second part.
Discuss any words or phrases you don't know.

A I paid for   second-class with no air conditioning.
But I ended up in   been cheated.
I really felt I had   first-class tickets in advance.

B Just after the plane   perform an emergency landing.
The pilot had to   down safely in the end.
But we made it   took off, we had engine trouble.

C When we were driving   for me.
One time we got stranded   across the country my friend kept gettir
It was the last straw   for directions all the time.
I got tired of stopping and asking   in a little town in the middle of nowhe

🎧 Now listen and check your answers.

👥 Have any of these travel experiences happened to you? What oth
kinds of experiences have you had while traveling?

■ Listening Task 👁 Look at the pictures. How is each person traveling?

1   2   3   4

1 First Listening

🎧 Listen to these people tell their travel stories. Check the true statements.

1.
☐ A farmer gave them clear directions.
☐ They got lost.

2.
☐ One of them pushed a cow.
☐ One of them pushed an Indian man.

3.
☐ She reserved a sleeping berth.
☐ She was traveling with an Italian man.

4.
☐ She was travel her mother.
☐ Her friends m. her.

2 Second Listening

🎧 Listen again. What is the story about?

1.
☐ getting lost
☐ going somewhere new

2.
☐ misunderstanding a custom
☐ the wrong place at the wrong time

3.
☐ not getting what you paid for
☐ depending on other people

4.
☐ feeling emba
☐ traveling by y

Real World Listening

1 Predict

Randy is in a travel agency in Thailand.
Why do you think he has ketchup all
over his shirt?

🎧 Now listen and check your prediction.

2 Get the main ideas

Put these events in order.

____ A van pulls up.

____ They arrive at the bus terminal.

____ Tim and Randy go to the travel agency.

____ Tim and Randy don't get on the van.

____ Tim and Randy get on the van.

____ Randy demands a taxi ride.

____ The woman squirts ketchup on Randy.

____ Randy gets angry at the travel agent.

____ Randy regrets his behavior.

3 Respond to the ideas

1. What do you think caused the misunderstanding between Randy and the travel agent?
2. Have you had a travel experience that you regretted or that you learned something from?

Language Awareness: Indefinite and definite nouns

🎧 **Listen and write the missing words.**

I had _a terrible airplane ride_ once. We had just taken off, and _____ suddenly blew up. The
flight attendants ran up and down _____ , and there was fire coming out of the engine. Then
_____ came on the intercom and said, in kind of _____ , "We're going to have to perform _____ , so let me explain what you'll need to do." We had to bend forward as far as we
could and wear our IDs for _____ . But after all, _____ was OK. We made it down safely,
and I was relieved.

Put each phrase where it belongs.

indefinite noun phrases
  a terrible airplane ride
  •
  •
  •

definite noun phrases
  • *the left engine*
  •
  •
  •

👤 Which of these nouns are definite because they refer to
things that are expected in the context?

INTERACTION LINK
*Swapping Travel
Stories*
➡ *page 60*

Real money

*If you had extra money,
what would you
do with it?
Save?
Spend?
Invest?*

■ Vocabulary Task

**Connect the first part of each sentence with the second part.
Discuss any words or phrases you don't know.**

A I have a lot of debts, especially | killing me.
And my tuition payments are | a get-rich-quick scheme.
I need to find | credit-card debt.

B I thought that buying and selling | it now, I'd lose a bundle.
I thought that real estate was one of | stocks was too risky.
So I bought a condo, but if I sold | the safest investments you could m

C I'm thinking about setting | to make more money than I'll ever r
I want to become | up an Internet business.
In fact, my goal is | that I want a worry-free future.
The bottom line is | financially independent.

🎧 Now listen and check your answers.

👥 Have you or someone you know ever tried to make a lot of money?
Did it work?

■ Listening Task 👁 What is each person's investment idea?

1 First Listening
🎧 What are these people doing to try to get money?

1. 　　　　　2. 　　　　　3. 　　　　　4.

2 Second Listening
🎧 Listen again. Do you think what they are doing is a good idea?

1. 　　　　　2. 　　　　　3. 　　　　　4.

Real World Listening

1 Predict

You are going to listen to a TV commercial for a product called "Real Money." **What do you think the commercial will be about?**

☐ real estate investments
☐ investing in the stock market
☐ starting your own company
☐ making money at home
☐ some other idea? _____

🎧 **Now listen and check your guess.**

2 Get the main ideas

Answer these questions.

1. How much money did the first woman make?
2. How many videos is he selling?
3. What is Steven Crowe's method for making money?
4. How much do his videos cost?
5. How do you order them?

3 Respond to the ideas

1. Who is Steven Crowe trying to sell his videos to?
2. Do you think it's easy to make money in real estate? Why or why not? Do you think it's possible to get rich quick?

Language Awareness: Countable and non-countable nouns

🎧 **Listen and write the missing words.**

I wanted to make a lot of ___*money*___ , so I decided to invest in _____ . I got _____ who really knows the market, and he helped me to find _____ . After a while, I made _____ , and was able to buy a house. Then I borrowed from my stock accounts to invest in _____ . To do that, I had to go into _____ . But then the real estate market crashed, and I lost everything. Now I can't pay my _____ . I guess I'll have to start all over again.

Put each phrase where it belongs.

singular countable nouns	plural countable nouns	non-countable nouns
a broker	• *stocks*	• *money*
•	•	•
	•	

👤 What is the difference in meaning between *I have a huge debt*, *I have a lot of debts*, and *I got into debt*?

INTERACTION LINK
You May Already Have Won!
➡ *page 62*

Never enough free time!

*How do you spend
your free time?
Do you have a hobby?
Do you belong
to any clubs?
Do you have enough
free time?*

■ Vocabulary Task

Connect the first part of each sentence with the second part.
Discuss any words or phrases you don't know.

A My personal time is
But I'm always
Give me my morning coffee
and my newspaper, and I'm

happy.
very important to me.
too lazy to do anything activ

B There's nothing like
Even if I have to listen to them
complain about
Only sometimes, it's

a drag.
their problems.
hanging out with good frier

C I have a long list of
It seems like I'm always way too busy with
I'm usually tired before
But every day I have to wake up and do

work.
projects I've got to get don
it all over again.
the day even starts.

🎧 Now listen and check your answers.

👥 Are you generally busy or do you have a lot of time to hang out? V
do you do with your time?

■ Listening Task 👁 Look at the pictures. What makes each person so busy?

1 *First Listening*

🎧 What do they want to do in their free time?

1. 2. 3. 4.

2 *Second Listening*

🎧 Listen again. Complete the expressions that the speakers use.

1. *All I want...* 2. *I couldn't imagine...* 3. *You wanna...* 4. *I've got to...*

Real World Listening

1 Predict

Carrie has a long commute to work. **What could she do on the commute?**

| ☐ read | ☐ listen to tapes | ☐ sleep | ☐ talk to other passengers | ☐ other |

🎧 Now listen and find out her friend's suggestions.

2 Get the main ideas

Read each statement. Write **T** for *True*, **F** for *False* or **?** for *no information*.

___ Carrie is tired.   ___ Carrie likes her commute.

___ Carrie is often late for work.   ___ Carrie loves living in the country.

___ Carrie's commute is less than an hour. ___ Carrie is looking for things to do on her commute.

3 Respond to the ideas

1. Do you think it's worth it for Carrie to live in the country?
2. Carrie says, "Sometimes it seems like my whole life is get up early, take the train, work all day, take the train home, go to bed, and then wake up and do it all over again." Do you ever feel that way? What do you do about it?

Language Awareness: Simple and phrasal modals

🎧 Listen and write the missing words.

A: Mike, you know you __*should*__ do your homework.

B: But Bill, I _____ to go out dancing with my girlfriend tonight.

A: But you _____ finish the report for history by tomorrow, or else your teacher _____ fail you ... remember?

B: But I _____ to go out dancing because she's mad at me and _____ start looking for someone else.

A: You know you _____ stay home and finish the report. You _____ be a good student.

B: Well, I'm going dancing. I think I _____ finish the report early tomorrow morning before class.

A: You just don't know how to use your time. You're really blowing it.

Put each phrase where it belongs.

Simple modals	phrasal modals	verbs
should	• have to	• want
	•	•
	•	

👥 Which of these modals mean obligation? Which mean possibility? Which mean ability?

INTERACTION LINK

Not Enough Money or Not Enough Time

➡ *page 63*

Disaster!

Have you ever been in a disaster? Or heard about a disaster? What happened?

■ Vocabulary Task

Connect the first part of each sentence with the second part.
Discuss any words or phrases you don't know.

A Health authorities | are being provided with clean drinking w
The disease | have reported an epidemic.
Residents | is spreading rapidly throughout the regi

B Hurricane Lydia has | left hundreds of people homeless.
The resulting floods have | declared a state of emergency.
The president has | devastated South Carolina.

C A volcano erupted | are being evacuated.
The military has been searching | in the Philippines.
Sadly, countless people | for survivors in the rubble.
Because of aftershocks, all remaining survivors | are missing.

🎧 Now listen and check your answers.

👥 Do you know anyone who has experienced a disaster like these? W
did the government do to help?

■ Listening Task 👁 Look at the pictures. What is the disaster?

1 First Listening

🎧 Listen to these fictional radio newscasts. What was the disaster? Where did it happe

1. 2. 3. 4.

2 Second Listening

🎧 Listen again. What is being done to help people?

1. 2. 3. 4.

Real World Listening

1 Predict

This is where Margaret used to live.
What happened?

🎧 Now listen and find out what happened.

2 Get the main ideas

Answer the questions.

1. When the earthquake hit, what did Margaret do?

   What did Julia do?

2. Why didn't Margaret and Julia go out the front door?

3. What happened to the first-floor apartment?

4. What happened to Mr. Sanchez?

   How do you know?

3 Respond to the ideas

1. How did Margaret and Julia feel about this experience?

2. Have you or anyone you know ever been in a disaster? How did they get through it? How did they feel about it afterward? Did it affect their lives in any way?

Language Awareness: Present perfect and present continuous

🎧 **Listen and write the missing words.**

1. An earthquake *has shaken* the city. The U.N. _____ food and water to help the survivors.

2. Floods _____ throughout the area. Residents _____ to leave the area immediately.

3. Because of an epidemic, hundreds of people _____ . The Red Cross _____ the country to help prevent the spread of disease.

4. A tornado _____ the city. The government _____ the military into the area to help with rescue efforts.

Put each phrase where it belongs.

present perfect	present continuous
has shaken	• *is supplying*
•	•
•	•
•	•

👥 Which tense is used to report what happened?
Which tense is used to report the response?

INTERACTION LINK

Emergency Aid

➡ *page 64*

Who needs advice?

Who do you ask when you need advice? Do other people often ask you for advice?

■ **Vocabulary Task**

Connect the first part of each sentence with the second part.
Discuss any words or phrases you don't know.

A My boss made me
But I'm afraid of telling him
I guess I don't know

what I think about it.
how to stand up for myself.
work overtime every day this week!

B I just can't seem to
And I've been
I guess I need to

see my doctor about an exercise plan.
lose weight.
having chest pains recently.

C How can I get my parents to
They're always
I don't get along with
Maybe I need to

them anymore.
yelling at me about everything.
move out of the house.
try and understand me?

🎧 Now listen and check your answers.

👥 Have you or someone you know ever had any of these problems? W
did you or that person do about it?

■ **Listening Task** 👁 What problems do these people have?

1 *First Listening*
🎧 What problems are the speakers talking about?

1.
2.
3.
4.

2 *Second Listening*
🎧 Listen again. What advice does Andrea Price give?

1.
2.
3.
4.

eal World Listening

Predict

hee is a Korean-American. She is calling for advice.
is planning to get married to a man from India.
at **do you think she wants advice about?**

whether she should marry him or not

how they should deal with her parents

how they should deal with his parents

whether they should have children

ome other issues? _____

Now listen and check your prediction.

Get the main ideas

ich statements describe Sunhee's problem?

Sunhee's parents live far away.

Sunhee wants to have a child.

Sunhee wants to get married.

☐ Sunhee's fiancé has a different religion.

☐ Sunhee's fiancé doesn't like her parents.

☐ Sunhee's parents want her to marry a Korean.

ich statements describe Carla's advice?

Do what your parents want.

Follow your heart.

☐ Have a child.

☐ Move back to your home country.

Respond to the ideas

Do you agree with Carla's advice? Would you give any different advice?
What are your views about international marriage?

anguage Awareness: Verbs plus prepositions

Listen and write the missing words.

This is Sports Talk, with Jim Steele. Caller, what's your problem?

I'm a baseball player on the university team, but I don't <u>**get along with**</u> my coach. He's always

_____ me, but I'm _____ confronting him. I'm _____ quitting the team.

So what's holding you back?

I can't quit really. I have an athletic scholarship that _____ my education.

Why don't you _____ him then? Tell him that you won't _____ the swearing anymore.

I don't really know how to _____ it with him.

t each phrase where it belongs.

nple verb + preposition	phrasal verb + preposition	adjective + preposition
• swearing at	• get along with	• afraid of
•	•	
•	•	

INTERACTION LINK

Advice Column

➡ *page 65*

What is the difference between a phrasal verb and a regular verb?

hich type is *holding you back*?

Fixing up the place

How do you like the place where you live? Do you wish you could fix it up?

■ **Vocabulary Task**

Connect the first part of each sentence with the second part.
Discuss any words or phrases you don't know.

A I want a room that is
I want a nice thick
I think I'd like to get an

braided rug and some lava lamps
overstuffed rattan chair.
soothing and relaxing, not sterile

B I want a room that is useful
I want to be able to work
I want lots of bookshelves

to hold all my books and papers.
for hanging out and studying.
on my computer in a comfortable

C I don't like my room
Right now, it's full of
I ought to get rid of
Then I could rearrange

a bunch of junk.
the way it is.
the furniture and make it more a
the junk and fix it up.

🎧 Now listen and check your answers.

👥 Which of these types of rooms is yours like? Would you like to changes?

■ **Listening Task** 👁 Look at the pictures. Describe each room.

1 First Listening

🎧 What are these people talking about doing to fix up their place?

1.   2.   3.   4.

2 Second Listening

🎧 Listen again. One person has an idea to fix up the place. What does the other per think about that idea? Check your answer.

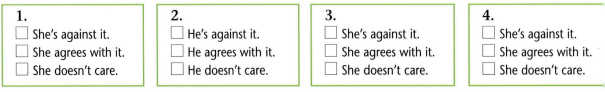

1.
☐ She's against it.
☐ She agrees with it.
☐ She doesn't care.

2.
☐ He's against it.
☐ He agrees with it.
☐ He doesn't care.

3.
☐ She's against it.
☐ She agrees with it.
☐ She doesn't care.

4.
☐ She's against it.
☐ She agrees with it.
☐ She doesn't care.

eal World Listening

Predict

ah and Richard are married university
dents. Look at this picture of their
artment. **What do you think they
ld do to fix up the place?**

Now listen and find out
r suggestions.

Get the main ideas

te **R** (Richard) or **S** (Sarah) or **X** (Neither) next to each statement or question.

___ A room is just a room.

___ I just want it to show our personalities.

___ I want to get a few things to make it feel
like it's our home.

___ I really like your idea!

___ How about a couple of psychedelic posters?

___ We don't have any time for parties.

___ I was thinking of a rattan chair and some
hanging plants.

___ At least we can agree on that.

Respond to the ideas

How are Sarah's and Richard's personalities different?
Do you agree with your family or roommates about how to fix up or decorate your home?
n what ways do you disagree?

anguage Awareness: Gerunds and bare verbs

Listen and write the missing words.

You know, Layla, I'm really tired of ___**being**___ surrounded by these four white walls. Why don't we
_____ some wallpaper up?

Oh, yuck, I don't think we should _____ wallpaper. How about _____ the walls instead?

I don't know… I want something more exciting than that. I was thinking of _____ a kind of tex-
tured wallpaper that you can paint over.

Hmm. I think we ought to _____ check it out. Let me see for myself what kind of
wallpaper you're talking about _____ .

You know, we could always _____ paint and then add texture with a sponge.

t each phrase where it belongs.

erunds

being

bare verbs

• *put*

•

•

•

What kind of words come before the gerunds?
hat kind of words come before the bare verbs?

INTERACTION LINK

Fixing Up the Place

➥ *page 67*

Losing someone

The loss of a loved one is a difficult thing to deal with. No one enjoys talking about a death in the family, but sometimes we need to.

■ Vocabulary Task

Connect the first part of each sentence with the second part.
Discuss any words or phrases you don't know.

A It's hard to deal with | how to make it through.
It leaves a big hole | the loss of someone you love.
Somehow, we learn | that no one else can fill up.

B Even though my father | tough on me.
He was hit by a car and | killed instantly.
It was really | passed away a long time ago, I still miss

C The doctors said it | is nothing more they can do.
They tried everything, but there | of things we did together.
My grandmother | could be any day now.
I have a lot of great memories | is ready to go — she just wants it to

🎧 Now listen and check your answers.

👥 Which of these situations do you think is easier to experience? Whi
is harder?

■ Listening Task 👁 Look at the pictures. Who is each person talking about?

1 First Listening
🎧 Check the true statements.

1.
☐ Yoshi's father passed away a long time ago.
☐ Yoshi's father died recently.

2.
☐ Liz's daughter was in an accident.
☐ Liz's daughter was in the hospital.

3.
☐ Tim's grandfather died in his sleep.
☐ Tim's grandfather died at home.

4.
☐ Lucy is gettir
☐ Lucy's condit getting wors

2 Second Listening
🎧 Listen again. What statements do the listeners use?

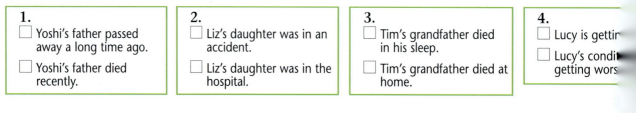

1. *I'm...*
2. *Poor...*
3. *I'm...*
4. *That must...*

I Real World Listening

1 Predict

A man is talking to someone about his late wife.
What do you think he will talk about?

☐ how they first met   ☐ how lonely he is

☐ her last few days   ☐ their children

☐ good times they had together   ☐ another topic?

🎧 **Now listen and check your prediction.**

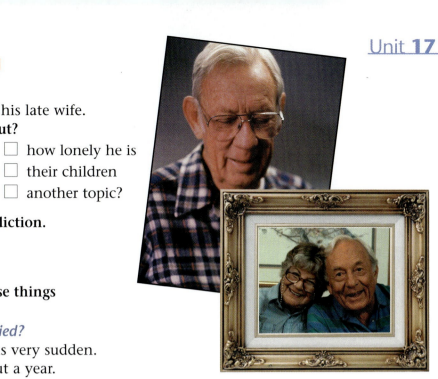

2 Get the main ideas

How does Mr. Hayes respond to these things that the host says?

1. Do you mind telling us how she died?

☐ **a.** She died in her sleep. It was very sudden.

☐ **b.** Cancer. She had it for about a year.

2. You get to know someone pretty well in 56 years, don't you?

☐ **a.** When they're gone, there's a big hole that no one can fill up

☐ **b.** Actually, you think you get to know them, but you really don't.

3. I imagine you have some wonderful memories, as well.

☐ **a.** We had a lot of good times, Maggie and me.

☐ **b.** I really don't feel like talking about it anymore.

3 Respond to the ideas

1. Mr. Hayes says, "You share so many years of your life with someone, and when they're gone, there's a big hole that no one can fill up." How do you think he could try to fill that hole? What could he do to ease his loneliness?

2. What could you do to help someone deal with the loss of a family member?

Language Awareness: Questions

🎧 **Listen and write the missing words.**

A: <u>_Did you_</u> hear about Annie? _____ terrible?

B: No, I didn't hear. _____?

A: Her mother passed away last night.

B: Oh no, _____ Mrs. Chun is gone? She was such a great lady. _____ die?

A: They don't really know _____ died. She just never woke up.

B: _____ seen Annie?

A: No, but she must be devastated. _____ do to help her?

B: There must be something we can do.

Put each phrase where it belongs.

yes-no questions	wh-questions	embedded questions
• *did you*	• *what happened*	• *how she*
•	•	
•	•	
•		

INTERACTION LINK

Who Would You Bring Back?

➡ *page 68*

👥 Which of these questions switch the subject and verb? Which do not? Why?

How can I help you?

Think of a store that has excellent service. What do they do that makes shopping there so enjoyable?

■ Vocabulary Task

Connect the first part of each sentence with the second part. Discuss any words or phrases you don't know.

A I'll be your waiter   proof that you're old enough.
Could I please see   this evening.
I can't serve you alcohol without   some ID?

B Could you take a look at   buying a new car at this time.
I'm not interested in   my car? It needs work.
I'm hoping you'll be able to   fix my old one.

C I really don't like being   the manager.
I thought it was possible to exchange   treated rudely like that.
I would like to remain   this or get a refund.
I think I need to speak to   a satisfied customer.

🎧 Now listen and check your answers.

👥 What stores have given you really good customer service? Have you ever been a salesperson or a waiter? What did you have to do to please the customer?

■ Listening Task 👁 Look at the pictures. What do you think the people are saying?

1 First Listening

🎧 Listen to these conversations between customers and sales or service people. What goods or services are they talking about?

1. _____ 2. _____ 3. _____ 4. _____

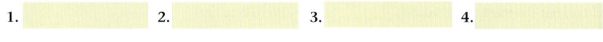

2 Second Listening

🎧 Listen again. Do the customers get what they want? Why or why not?

1. _____ 2. _____ 3. _____ 4. _____

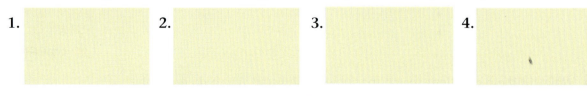

eal World Listening

Predict

ustomer is returning
hirt to a store.
at do you think
h person will say?

the customer
- ☐ Is it possible to exchange this shirt?
- ☐ This shirt is stained! I want my money back!

the manager
- ☐ I'm very sorry about any problems there may have been.
- ☐ What's the problem?

the clerk
- ☐ Are you sure you didn't do it?
- ☐ Let me see how we can help you.

Now listen and
ck your prediction.

Get the main ideas

wer these questions.

What does the customer want to do?

According to the customer, how did the shirt get stained?

According to the clerk, how did the shirt get stained?

When the manager comes, what does the customer say he wants to do?

What does the customer end up doing?

Respond to the ideas

Do you think this situation happens often in stores? Why or why not?

Have you ever asked to speak to a manager in a store or restaurant? Or have you had any
other kind of bad experience with service? What happened?

anguage Awareness: Noun clauses as objects

Listen and write the missing words.

I'm _wondering_ what I should do about my motorcycle. The engine keeps stalling. Can you fix it?

Well, it _____ like you'll need to leave it for an inspection.

It's at home right now. I'm _____ if I can bring it in later today?

Well, I can't _____ that we'll get to it today, but we'll look at it as soon as we can. However, I need
proof that you're old enough to drive a motorcycle. _____ like you're under 18.

Are you _____ that if I'm not 18 yet, I can't get my motorcycle fixed? I don't _____ that I want to
bring it here, after all. But I don't _____ where else I can go.

t each phrase where it belongs.

rb + *wh*-clause	verb + *if*-clause	verb + *like*-clause	verb + *that*-clause
wondering	• wondering	• sounds	• guarantee
		•	•
			•

INTERACTION LINK

And the Service is Great!

➡ *page 69*

Which of these verbs refer to *thinking*?
nich refer to *perceiving*? Which refer to *communicating*?

Putting food on the table

Do you enjoy cooking? How hard is it for you to find things to cook?

■ Vocabulary Task

Connect the first part of each sentence with the second part. Discuss any words or phrases you don't know.

A I need to pick up something | quick and easy.
I'd like to be able to throw together something | and toss it in the microwave.
The easiest would be to just open up a package | for dinner on the way home.

B What's for dinner? Instant noodles | for pizza.
I'm so sick | again?
I guess I'll have to order out | of that junk.

C I'm hoping to get | something to eat every single d
It's hard to find | a decent, well-balanced meal.
There's never enough | a care package from Mom soor
I wish someone would cook me | ingredients in the fridge to make

🎧 Now listen and check your answers.

👥 What kind of food do you usually eat for dinner? Which meals ◄ you like the most?

■ Listening Task 👁 Look at the pictures. What are these people going to eat

1 First Listening

🎧 What do they decide to eat for dinner?

1. 2. 3. 4.

2 Second Listening

🎧 Listen again. Who is going to make or buy the dinner tonight?

1. 2. 3. 4.

Real World Listening

1 Predict

Look at the picture.
Tony and Rob are two university students who are sharing an apartment. Tony just received a package from his mother. **What do you think will be in the package?**

🎧 Now listen and check your prediction.

a sweater

a letter and photos

a cookbook

cookies

the things Tony left at home

a lot of fruit

2 Get the main ideas

1. What did Tony get in the mail from his mom?

2. What do Tony and Rob usually do for dinner?

3. What do they have in their refrigerator and kitchen cabinets?

4. What are they going to get at the supermarket?

5. What do they eat for dinner?

3 Respond to the ideas

1. Do you think Rob and Tony will use the cookbook much? Why or why not?

2. Rob says, "What we really need is for you to find a girlfriend who can cook." Why did he say that? How do you feel about it?

3. Who does the cooking at your place? If it's you, how difficult is it to cook and also balance all the other things you do? If you don't cook, do you help out? How?

Language Awareness: Interrogative (wh-) clauses

🎧 **Listen and write the missing words.**

A: What are you making for dinner tonight?

B: Nothing. You __*know*__ what an awful cook I am.

A: Well, I thought I'd ask. What's in the fridge _____ pretty awful.

B: Yeah, there's pretty much nothing.

A: Well, that's depressing. What we really need around here _____ a professional cook.

B: Let's think _____ what to do. Should we take cooking lessons?

A: Do you have any _____ how much time it takes to cook? We can't go to school full-time and be cooks, too.

B: I'm just tired _____ what I have to eat every day.

A: Well, we'll just have to _____ whatever is easy, no _____ how bad it tastes.

Put each phrase where it belongs.

verb + wh-clause as subject	verb + wh-clause as object	preposition + wh-clause as object	noun + wh-clause
• *looks*	• *know*	• *about*	• *idea*
•	•		
•			

👥 Draw brackets around each wh-clause. How can you tell where it begins and ends?

INTERACTION LINK
Cook or Eat Out?

➡ *page 70*

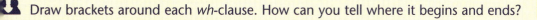

Breaking news

Do you watch the news regularly? Have you seen the news channels report "breaking news" as soon as something important happens?

■ Vocabulary Task

Connect the first part of each sentence with the second part. Discuss any words or phrases you don't know.

A An incredible breakthrough in
Scientists have learned how
For the first time in history, successful

experiments were performed on human patients.
medicine has just been revealed.
to eradicate genetic heart disease in hu

B We just learned that the military
We attempted to question military personnel
We will have an update

but they could not be reached for comm
when we get more details.
has accidentally destroyed a vital strate site.

C Those two countries are
They are
The region has been
The U.N. is

planning to send a peacekeeping force and intervene.
at it again.
flexing their muscles, trying to intimid each other.
under dispute for years.

🎧 Now listen and check your answers.

👥 **What has happened in each of these stories? Do you know of any recent news events like these? What happened?**

■ Listening Task 👁 Look at the pictures. What kind of news story is it?

1 First Listening

🎧 Listen to these imaginary news clips. Check the true statements.

1.
☐ The World Series will be played in Japan.
☐ Three teams will participate.

2.
☐ Some people have been killed in a school.
☐ The suspect has not been caught.

3.
☐ A new drug has been developed for university students.
☐ The drug promises a cure for heart disease.

4.
☐ Two nation over owner region.
☐ The nation reach an a

2 Second Listening

🎧 Listen to the news clips again. Write down some additional details.

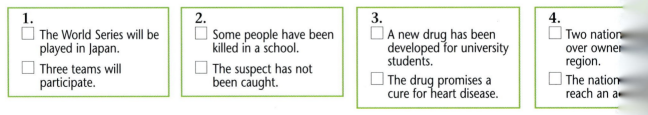

1.   2.   3.   4.

eal World Listening

Predict

o friends are discussing a news
ry about a conflict between
o countries.

at conflict do you think
y might talk about?

- ☐ Religious persecution
- ☐ Border conflicts
- ☐ Trade dispute
- ☐ Fishing rights
- ☐ Human rights violations

Now listen and check your prediction.

Get the main ideas

Listen again.

Are David and Nehal worried about the situation?

Why or why not?

Do Nehal and David think the U.N. should get involved?

Respond to the ideas

Nehal said, "India and Pakistan do not care about Kashmir." "All they care about is fighting
with each other." Do you think she is right? Why or why not?

What do you think about nuclear weapons? Should they be banned? Or are they important
or keeping peace?

Do you think the United Nations should mind its own business, or be an active peacekeeper?

anguage Awareness: Active and passive verbs

1 Listen and write the missing words.

tounding events have just been __*revealed*__ by the U.S. government. Apparently, in 1947 in New
exico, experiments were _____ on alien creatures that _____ into the desert in their
acecraft. The aliens _____ the crash, but were _____ to a top-secret facility. While at the
cility, they were _____ to radiation treatments and a variety of diseases, in order to determine
eir resistance. The aliens _____ as a result of the experiments, and their bodies were
_____ in underground vaults to preserve them for future research.

t each phrase where it belongs.

ctive verbs	passive verbs	
• crashed	• revealed	•
	•	•
	•	

2 How do you know which verbs are passive?

r each passive verb, who is doing the action?

INTERACTION LINK

Repercussions

➡ *page 71*

47

INTERACTION LINKS

Work with your classmates.
Do one activity after you finish each unit.

INTERACTION LINK

Life Choices

1. Form groups of three or four.
2. Roll a die  or, if you don't have dice, use the number grid on page 72.
   Find your number below and talk about the choices. Tell which you would choose and explain why. Does everyone in your group agree?

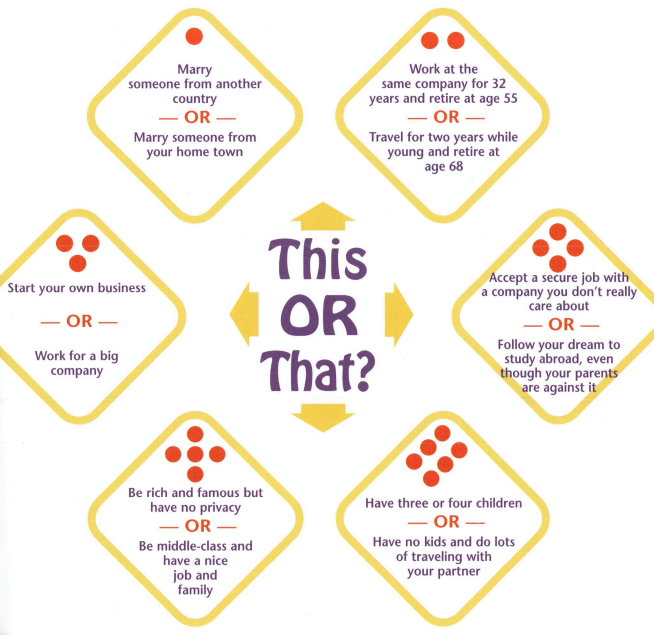

Marry
someone from another
country
— OR —
Marry someone from
your home town

Work at the
same company for 32
years and retire at age 55
— OR —
Travel for two years while
young and retire at
age 68

Start your own business
— OR —
Work for a big
company

Accept a secure job with
a company you don't really
care about
— OR —
Follow your dream to
study abroad, even
though your parents
are against it

Be rich and famous but
have no privacy
— OR —
Be middle-class and
have a nice
job and
family

Have three or four children
— OR —
Have no kids and do lots
of traveling with
your partner

This
OR
That?

OPTIONS

Add your own "this or that" choices to the chart. Discuss them.

Look again at the choices. What are the possible good and bad results of each?

Who Are You Really?

1. Form groups of three to five people.

2. Take turns. Choose a box and think of something about your life. Then read the box aloud.

3. Others in your group ask yes/no questions to try to guess what this aspect of your life is. If they cannot guess after asking 20 questions, tell them the answer.

4. Tell your group more details about it. Your group members can ask about things that are interesting about it.

5. Continue until you have done all the boxes, or until time is up.

Something I'm good at now	Something I'm bad at (but I love doing it anyway)	Something I collect (or used to collect)	A special trip	Something I liked doing with my family
Something I like to do with my friends	Something I like to do by myself	A restaurant I love	A book that taught me something special	Someone who inspired me
Something I used to want to be	A job I've had	A dream I had when I was in high school	Something active I like to do	Something quiet I like to do
A pet	A special friendship	A talent I have (or used to have)	Something I hate having to do	Three verbs that say something about me
Three nouns that say something about me	Three adjectives that say something about me	A home (or place) I've lived in	A special place in my city	A school I attended

HINT FOR ASKING QUESTIONS:
Start with general questions and work toward more specific details.

Complain About...

1. Form groups of three or four. Everyone rolls a die (or use the number grid on page 72 if you don't have dice) and the person with the lowest number goes first.

2. In turns, roll the die and move your token the number of spaces you rolled. Complain about the person, place or thing in the space where you land. Your partners should make comments, and maybe give advice.

3. The next person rolls the dice, moves her token the correct number of spaces, and complains about whatever is in that space.

4. Continue around the board until someone is first to reach the end (or, go around twice if you have lots of complaints).

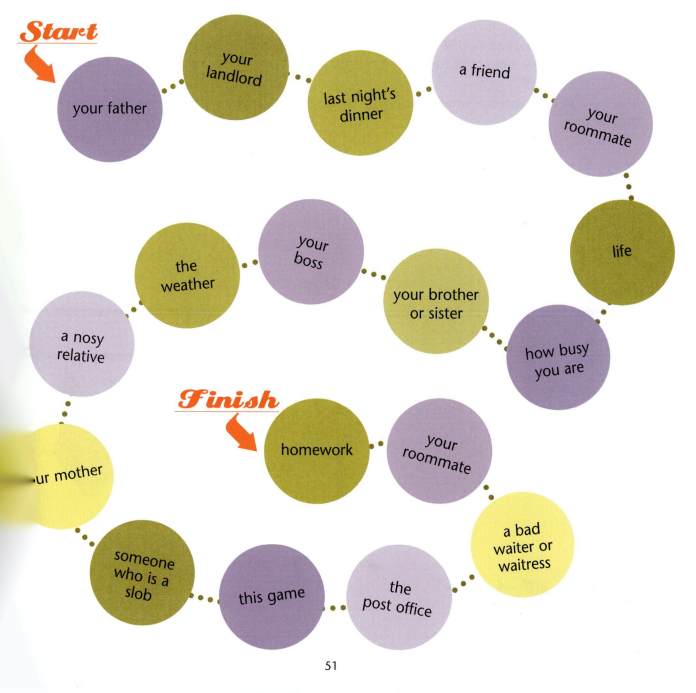

Start

your father · your landlord · last night's dinner · a friend · your roommate · life · your brother or sister · how busy you are · your boss · the weather · a nosy relative · your mother · someone who is a slob · this game · the post office · a bad waiter or waitress · your roommate · homework

Finish

Design a Wardrobe

1. **Form groups of three or four. Each group chooses a different one of the following:**
    - one of your teachers
    - one of your classmates
    - someone famous
    - yourself

    Your task is to design a wardrobe for that person using a limited amount of money.

2. **Roll a die or use the number grid on page 72. The numbers below show the amount of money you can spend on a wardrobe for your person:**

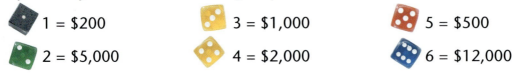

    1 = $200   3 = $1,000   5 = $500

    2 = $5,000   4 = $2,000   6 = $12,000

3. **Talk for 15 minutes and decide what clothes you will buy for your person. Try to use all the money. Talk about what colors are good for the person you chose, what fabrics, what styles, and what patterns.**

4. **Share your ideas with the whole class. Who did each group choose? What kind of wardrobe did they design?**

ITEM	Discount Store	Medium Fashion Store	High Fashion Designer Store	Details *(what colors, fabrics, styles & patterns)*
Footwear (shoes, sandals, boots, etc.)	$25/pair (x ____)	$100/pair (x ____)	$500/pair (x ____)	_____
Jeans	$25/pair (x ____)	$50/pair (x ____)	$100/pair (x ____)	_____
Shorts	$15/pair (x ____)	$30/pair (x ____)	$75/pair (x ____)	_____
Hats	$10 (x ____)	$35 (x ____)	$200 (x ____)	_____
Women's Dresses	$30 (x ____)	$100 (x ____)	$350 (x ____)	_____
Women's Skirts	$30 (x ____)	$50 (x ____)	$300 (x ____)	_____
Women's Blouses	$25 (x ____)	$50 (x ____)	$200 (x ____)	_____
Women's Suits	$100 (x ____)	$300 (x ____)	$1,000 (x ____)	_____
Men's Slacks	$35 (x ____)	$100 (x ____)	$300 (x ____)	_____
Men's Dress Shirts	$25 (x ____)	$50 (x ____)	$150 (x ____)	_____
Men's Casual Shirts	$15 (x ____)	$35 (x ____)	$75 (x ____)	_____
Other: _____	$____ (x ____)	$____ (x ____)	$____ (x ____)	_____
Other: _____	$____ (x ____)	$____ (x ____)	$____ (x ____)	_____

TYPES OF FABRICS, STYLES AND PATTERNS

Fabrics: cotton, polyester, silk, satin, wool, denim, lace

Styles: casual, designer, sporty, formal

Patterns: plain, striped, plaid, checked, with polka dots, with a ___ print
(for example, with a surfboard print)

Which English?

1. **Form three or four teams. The teacher gives each team one of these four statements:**
   a. British English should be taught as the standard.
   b. American English should be taught as the standard.
   c. Countries (or schools) should choose which they will teach as a standard from among the following three Englishes: British, American and Australian.
   d. Each country uses its own version of English as its own standard (for example, Indian English in India, Singaporean English in Singapore).

2. **Everyone is given 15-20 minutes to prepare their arguments.**

3. **Starting with Team 1, each team is given 3 minutes to present their stance and support their arguments.**
   Then each team will get 2 minutes to argue against the other two teams' ideas.
   Finally each team gets 1 minute to sum up.

Matchmakers

A "matchmaker" is a person who helps two other people get together for a date. When neither person has seen the other, this is called a "blind date."

1. **Make groups of four. In each group, make two pairs — Pair A and Pair B.**

2. **Pair A and Pair B separate, so neither pair can hear what the other is saying. Fill out a "profile sheet" (see below) for a possible blind date person for the other pair. Try to make your profile appealing to the people in the other pair.**

3. **Get back into your groups of four.**
   Pair A: introduce your "profile person" to Pair B.
   Pair B: ask questions about the person.

4. **Pair B decides if either of them (or one of their friends or relatives) would like to go on a blind date with this "profile person."**

5. **Do the same thing with Pair B's "profile person."**

Blind Date Profile Sheet

Age _____   Residence _____

Occupation _____   Salary _____

Likes / Dislikes about the job _____

Height _____   Weight _____   Body Type _____

Personality (good and bad) _____

Hobbies _____

Preferences	Favorite	Least Favorite
Music		
Movies		
Reading material		
TV programs		
Sports		
Food		
Clothing		

Favorite places to go on a date _____

This person's idea of a perfect romantic evening _____

_____

Pet peeves _____

Family Lies

1. On the chart below, fill in just four members of your family — choose any four, and write something unusual about that each person. Then add a fifth member that you make up. This fifth member is not a real member of your family. The goal is to fool your partner so that he or she can't guess which ones are real members of your family and which one is made up.

2. Get into groups of 3 or 4. Take turns introducing the members of your family. After you finish introducing all five people (including the fictitious member), your groupmates can ask questions to try to discover which person is not really a member of your family. You have to tell the truth about the real members of your family, but you can lie about the fictitious member. Try to tell lies that will convince your partners that the made-up member is really part of your family.

3. After each group member has asked 2-3 questions, they guess which member is not really in your family. Tell which member is not real.

4. Repeat Steps 2 and 3 with the next member in your group, and continue until everyone has talked about their families.

OPTION:

After finishing, talk about the relationships among your family members, using some of the phrases you learned in this unit.

	Name	An interesting fact about them
Mother (or stepmother)		
Father (or stepfather)		
Sister		
Brother		
Grandmother		
Grandfather		
Aunt		
Uncle		
Niece		
Nephew		
Daughter		
Son		
?		
?		

What's Bugging You?

You will interview someone from a different culture to find out more about cultural differences.

If You Are In Your Home Country

1. Interview at least one foreign person who is living in your country. (If there are very few foreign people living in your town or city, you could interview a foreign teacher.) Your job is to find something that bothers the person about living in your country. Some useful things to find out:

    *   What is it exactly that bothers them?
    *   Why does it bother them?
    *   Is it something that is done differently in their home country? If so, how is it different? Or is it something that isn't done at all in their country?
    *   Is it something they connect with your culture, or just with living in the country?
    *   Is it something that only some people do, or is it something that most people in your culture do?

2. If you have a chance, try to explain why it's done the way it is done in your country. See if you can help the other person to understand this aspect of living in your country.

3. Back in class, share what you learned in groups of three or four.

    Discuss:
    *   Is the thing that bothers this person really cultural, or is it more of an individual thing?
    *   If it's cultural, why is it done like that? Why wouldn't it make sense to someone from a different culture?

4. Share what you learned with the rest of the class. What cultural differences did each group talk about? Were the things mentioned really cultural, or individual?

If You Are In a Different Country

.   In class, make groups of three or four. Discuss things that bug you about living in this country, especially things you think are cultural differences. Have other people noticed the same things, or are you the only one who seems to have noticed this? Do you all agree that this is probably a cultural difference and not an individual thing that only a few people in the country do?

Choose one thing in particular that bugs you. Then, outside of class, interview a local person (that is, if you are in Australia, interview an Australian). Your job is to find out why this thing is done this way. See if you can find a reason that makes sense to you.

Back in class, discuss what you learned in groups of three or four.

Share what you learned with the rest of the class. What cultural differences did each group talk about? Were the things mentioned really cultural, or individual?

NT: How to Begin

saying something like this: "I'm a student at _____. [school name] We're doing a search project about understanding cultural differences. If you don't mind, I'd like to ask you some estions ..."

INTERACTION LINK

Future Toys

1. Make groups of three or four. What kinds of inventions would you most like to see in the future? Brainstorm ideas for several different future inventions. *

2. Talk about three or four of your dream toys and what they can do.

3. Then choose one of your group's ideas and discuss more specific details of what it can do.

4. Design a radio or TV ad for your invention, like the ads in the "Listening Task" section of Unit 9.

5. Each group presents their ad to the class. What inventions did each group talk about? Which ones would you buy?

* Can't think of anything? How about smellivision or an instant teleporter?

OPTIONS:
- record all groups' ads on cassette or video, if there is access to equipment
- make print ads
- design websites

Kick the Habit

1. Get in groups of three or four. Everyone rolls a die and the person with the lowest number goes first. If you don't have dice, use the number grid on page 72.
2. Roll the dice and move your token the number of spaces you rolled. Say whether you know a man or a woman who does this or not (don't say any names). If not, roll again. If yes, describe this person's habit. Then let your partners offer advice about how this person can quit.
3. Continue around the board until the last person reaches the end (or, go around twice).

Swapping Travel Stories

Almost everybody has either a horror story or a funny story about traveling. What's yours?

1. Think of a travel story you want to tell. (If you don't have a travel story, think of a story about a time you got in trouble with your parents, or an embarrassing story.)

2. Look at the story-telling hints and plan how to tell your story.

3. Form groups of three or four. Everyone tells their stories. Other group members can ask questions.

4. Think about how you told your story, and how you can change it to make it better (usually, stories get better and better each time we tell them).
    HINT: The questions your group members asked can give you some good ideas for details to add to your story.

5. Get into new groups of three or four. Everyone tells his or her story again.

Story-Telling Hints

1. **BE WELL ORGANIZED**

   A. **Begin by getting your audience's attention**, like "I had a really funny experience in Bangkok" or "I had a terrible airplane ride once."

   B. **Set the beginning scene** (when, where, who and what).
      1. When did it happen?
      2. Where were you?
      3. Who were the main characters at the beginning?
      4. What was happening at the time the story begins?

   C. **Tell what happens next** (in addition to telling what happens, be sure to introduce any changes in when, where and who.)

   D. **Add dialogue** — it's usually more interesting than just a narration.

   E. **At the end, say something that shows what you learned or how you felt** about what happened, like "I felt terrible, I wished I could apologize" or "I couldn't eat for two days."

2. **BE AN ANIMATED STORY-TELLER**

   A. **Vary your voice.**
      1. Change your tone, from high to low, depending on what's happening in the story.
      2. Change volume — sometimes louder, sometimes softer, sometimes even a whisper.
      3. Change speed — speak faster when there's action, and speak slower (or even pause) to build suspense.
      4. Character voices — change your voice to try to sound like the character in the story.

   B. **Sound effects** — make sounds that fit what's happening (knocking on doors, footsteps, etc.).

   C. **Facial expression** — use your face to help tell the story, by showing fear, happiness, sadness, love, etc.

   D. **Body movement and gestures**
      1. To add effect, sometimes move closer to your audience (for example, when you whisper), or farther away.
      2. Do the body movements that your story's characters are doing.
      3. Use gestures when it seems to fit the story.

   E. **Make eye contact with your audience.**

You May Already Have Won!

CONGRATULATIONS! You may already have won $3,000,000!
That's right. If you are the person with the winning number, you will win $3 million.
What will you do with all that money? Invest? Take a trip? Buy a house?

Here are the lucky numbers to choose from. One of these will be the big winner.

TS7085	RH1019
SB4224	AQ7229
MR5598	RS5078
YM1162	MM3718

1. Form groups of three or four. Choose one of the eight lucky numbers (each group must have a different number). Write your number on a piece of paper (this will be your lucky ticket) and put all the tickets into a box.

2. Your job is to decide how you will spend the $3 million if you win. You have to agree on how to invest and spend the money. The only rules are:
   - You cannot divide it evenly among your group members — you have to decide together how to spend it.
   - You have to use at least three different kinds of investments (you cannot just put the money in a bank account). However, you can choose how risky you want your investments to be.
   - You have to spend part of it for something fun.

3. At the end of the game, somebody (for example, your teacher) chooses one of the tickets from the box and announces the winning number. The winners tell about how they agreed to use the money. What did they decide? Would you do the same thing?

Not Enough Money or Not Enough Time

1. Form groups of three or four. One student rolls a die or uses the number grid on page 72, then checks the number on the chart below.

NUMBER	How Much Money You Have Free	How Much Time You Have Free
1	$25 per week	1 weekday evening and 3 hours on the weekends
2	$150 per week	2 weekday mornings (you work afternoons and evenings)
3	$5 per week	every weekday evening and all day on Saturdays
4	$50 per week	all day on Sundays
5	$15 per week	all weekend
6	$2,000 for a vacation	one week of vacation, with two weekends

2. Each of the other group members suggests an activity to do with the amount of money and amount of free time you rolled. After each group member has suggested a free-time activity, decide which one you would do and explain why.

3. Continue to the next person in your group. (If you roll a number that has already been done, roll again).

OPTION:

Groups are assigned one of the numbers by the teacher. Discuss ways of using your money and time — your group has to agree on activities to do together.

Emergency Aid

1. **Form groups of four or five. Choose one of these disasters:**
   - a volcano eruption in the Philippines
   - an earthquake in northern China in January
   - floods in Queensland, Australia, in December
   - a typhoon in Hong Kong

2. **Your group's job is to send a cargo plane full of emergency aid items to the disaster area. However, the plane has only enough room for five big boxes, and each box can have only one kind of item. Discuss what aid items are most important. (You have to agree on which five items are most important for the survivors of the disaster.)**

Blankets	Toilet paper	Canned food	Bottled water	Bandages
Can openers	Shoes	Soap/shampoo	Toothpaste/ toothbrushes	Candles/matches
Rope	Books	Cooking utensils	Flashlights	Gas stoves
Sunscreen	Pencils/paper	Baby formula	Aspirin	Diapers
your idea: _____	your idea: _____	your idea: _____	your idea: _____	your idea: _____

3. **Each group explains its decisions to the whole class. What disasters took place? What items di each group send?**

Advice Column

1. Form groups of three or four. Everyone rolls a die or uses the number grid on page 72 to get a number. The person with the lowest number goes first.

2. Take turns rolling the dice or using the number grid, and move your token the number of spaces you roll. Find the advice letter with the number you landed on.

3. Read the request for advice. Pretend you are the person with the problem. Your group members can ask you for more details about the problem (you have to make up the additional information).

4. Each group member gives you some advice. Decide whose advice you will follow and tell why.

5. Continue with the next person in your group.

6. When you land on a problem that was already done, move to the next one.

7. Continue taking turns until you have done most of the spaces, or until time is up.

please see next page >

I wish I knew what to do…

I don't know if we should…

It bothers me that…

I'm worried because…

< continued from previous page

Start →

1

I'm already too busy at work, but my boss just asked me to help with a new project. I'll go crazy if I have to do it, but I don't want to look like I can't handle extra responsibility. What should I do?
Signed, Stressed out

2

My buddies and I go out every weekend. They always choose me to be the designated driver, which means I can never drink anything. I'm not an alcoholic, but sometimes I like to have a few drinks, too. How can I get them to be fair and take turns?
Signed, Driving Me Crazy

3

We just found out my mother has stomach cancer. The doctor won't tell her— he says knowing the truth would be devastating. Should we tell my mother so she can make the most of her last days?
Signed, Wondering

Finish
↓

10

I bought a cassette on how to get rich in real estate, and I found out that it doesn't help at all. I feel like I was cheated, and I want my money back. When I called their office, though, they said, "All sales are final." What can I do?
Signed, Angry and broke

4

I just got accepted at the University of Melbourne, in Australia. My boyfriend is going to college in my home country. I don't want to live apart from him, but this is my chance to study abroad. What should I do?
Signed, Studious but in love

9

I go to college in the U.S. My teacher gave me a 'C' on my final paper, and gave an 'A' to a native speaker of English whose paper had a lot less information. I think he gave me a bad grade only because of some grammar mistakes. It doesn't seem fair. What can I do?
Signed, Victim of prejudice

5

My wife and I keep arguing about furniture, and it seems like we'll never agree on the same things. Should we each choose what we like, even if it doesn't match?
Signed, Sitting on a bare floor

8

My sister gave me an expensive designer blouse, but it's really not my style, and the color is awful. How can I exchange it without hurting her feelings?
Signed, Fashion-conscious

7

Two different people asked me to marry them. One is gentle, funny and easy to get along with. The other isn't quite as nice — but he makes twice as much money and wants to take care of me. Which should I marry?
Signed, Confused

6

My brother is a real slob. He leaves stuff all over. I'm embarrassed to have friends come over and see our home. What should I about it?
Signed, Tired of picking up

Fixing Up the Place

1. **Get into pairs. Choose one of the following situations:**
   - You are two university roommates.
   - You are a married couple who now have a new baby.
   - You are two friends who are both working.
   - You are a married couple, both going to university.

2. **Your job is to fix up your 2-bedroom apartment. Here is what your apartment looks like:**

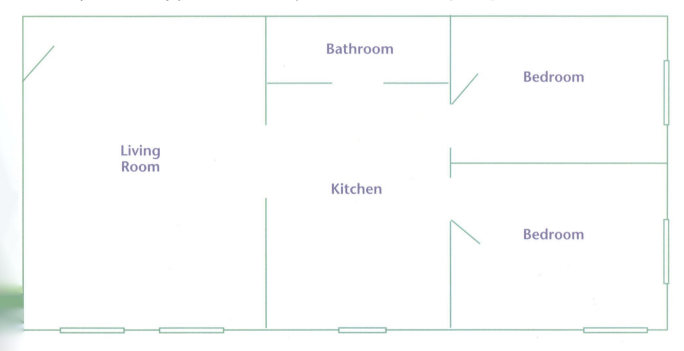

3. **Discuss how to fix up your place. Which room or rooms? What kinds of changes will you make? Will you get furniture? Plant, or posters or other decorations? Do you want to paint rooms? What colors? Do you need a computer, or other supplies? Do you want to remodel your kitchen or your bathroom?**

4. **You have to agree on five things to do to fix up your place.**

. **Each group reports to the whole class about how they decided to fix up their place, and why. What kinds of changes did each group choose?**

Who Would You Bring Back?

If you could bring one famous person from history back to life, who would it be?

1. **Make groups of 3 or 4. Discuss who you think would be the 10 best people to bring back, and why.**

2. **Of these 10 people, discuss and decide who would be the five best people to bring back, and why. Your group has to agree on who they would be.**

3. **Of these five people, discuss and decide who would be the best person to bring back, and why. Your group has to agree on who it would be.**

4. **Share your results with the whole class. Who did each group choose?**

OPTIONS:

1. What questions would you ask this person? Each group member can ask 1-2 questions. What do you think they would say as an answer to your questions?

2. What do you think this person would do if they were alive today?

3. Each person in the group tells about someone you knew personally and would like to bring back to life. Tell what was great about this person, and why this person was special to you.

And the Service is Great!

What are qualities of great service? How is it different for different businesses?

1. **Make groups of 3 or 4. Roll a die or use the number grid on page 72 to pick a kind of business:**

1. a medium-priced restaurant

2. a car repair shop

3. a clothing store

4. a toy store

5. a fast food restaurant

6. a computer and software store

2. **Decide as a group which three qualities are the most important for the type of business you rolled.**
    *   they're friendly
    *   they're polite
    *   they're attentive
        (for example, they notice that you are there, even if it's not your turn yet)
    *   they help you with what you want, rather than trying to get you to buy something you don't really need
    *   they're informed
        (they know about their product, and explain about options)
    *   they serve customers quickly and efficiently
    *   other _____
    *   other _____
    *   other _____

    Compare your results with other groups.

PTION:

esign a survey about a specific type of business you are interested in, to find out what service qualities are
ost important to customers of this kind of business. As homework, each member of your group ask the
rvey questions to 5 people (if you are in your home country, it's OK to ask people using your first lan-
age). Afterward, compare your results. Discuss what you discovered about what makes good service.

Cook or Eat Out?

1. Make groups of 3 or 4. Everyone roll the die, and the person with the lowest number goes first. (If you don't have dice, use the number grid on page 72.)

2. Take turns. Before you roll the die for your turn, say whether you will cook or eat out. Then roll the die and move your token the number of spaces you rolled. Read the situation for the place you landed. Then discuss what you would cook (if cooking) or what restaurant in your city you would go to, what you would order, and why. Other group members can suggest other ideas.

3. Keep going around the board until you've talked about all the situations, or until time is up.

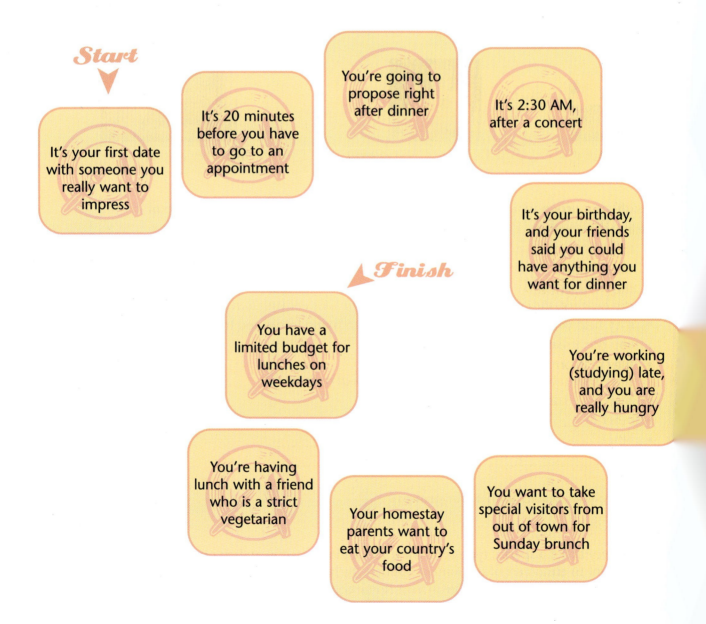

Repercussions

1. Make groups of 3 or 4. Decide how likely each news event is, using this scale:

    1 = impossible
    2 = not very likely
    3 = it might happen
    4 = it will definitely happen sometime soon

    You have to agree on your choices. If you disagree, discuss why you think you are right.

2. Discuss the repercussions of each item: How would it change our lives if it really happened?

1 2 3 4   Cure for Cancer Found!

1 2 3 4   Women Defeat Men in Pro Soccer Championship!

1 2 3 4   Alcohol Illegal!

1 2 3 4   U.S. Passes Gun Control Laws!

1 2 3 4   World Series Opened Up to Teams From Around the World!

1 2 3 4   Colonies Established on Mars!

2 3 4   Dollar Becomes World Currency!

2 3 4   U.S. gets First African–American President!

Share your answers with other groups, or with the whole class. What ideas did each group have?

Number Grid

This number grid may be used instead of a die or pair of dice.

Take turns closing your eyes and pointing to a number on this grid. Use the number that your finger lands on.

2	4	1	6	3
5	1	3	2	4
6	4	5	1	3
1	6	2	3	5
2	5	4	1	6

Self Study Pages

Real World Listening

Listen to the conversation. Fill in the missing parts.

can't believe it	have you been doing	Something like 20 years	treated you well
focus on my family	know what happened	start a family	what about you
get stuck being a	left to start	start my career	you haven't had any time
got a job	majored in marketing	too busy with school	
had our children	never too late	travel around Europe	
have my own	put him through	travel the world	

Sharon: Hey, Karen, is that you?

Karen: Sharon, wow! I _____ ! Yes, it's me. Gosh, it's good to see you!

Sharon: You, too! What's it been? _____ ?

Karen: Yeah, I can't believe we're that old already.

Sharon: Life sure has _____ . You look great!

Karen: Thanks, you do, too! What _____ all this time? I remember you couldn't wait to marry Jim and _____ .

Sharon: Hah! I never did get married. I was _____ and then my job. I don't even _____ to Jim.

Karen: So what do you do?

Sharon: I _____ advertising agency.

Karen: Come on, Sharon! You?

Sharon: Really. I _____ in college and afterwards _____ with an advertising agency. I worked my way up , and when I felt I understood the business really well, I _____ my own agency.

Karen: Wow, that's pretty impressive. No wonder _____ to get married.

Sharon: Yeah. So, anyway, _____ ? You were the one who was going to _____ and do your own thing. You didn't want to _____ housewife.

Karen: Hah! You're going to laugh, but I am a housewife, and a mother of three.

Sharon: Oh, come on, Karen, you're not serious, are you? What happened to the travel?

Karen: Well, I did _____ for a year with some friends. But then I met Stan, and we got married right away. I helped _____ medical school, and then we _____ . I love being able to _____ and when they leave home, I'm going to _____ — if it's not too late!

Sharon: It's _____ .

BONUS QUESTION

Imagine you are Karen or Sharon. Write a journal entry describing your meeting with your old school friend.

Real World Listening

Listen to the conversation. Choose the correct words.

Cesar: TJ, my man! I heard you won the Pro-Am (a) snowboarding (b) skateboarding contest last weekend.

TJ: Yeah, Cesar, I did a flip on the half-pipe that really (a) depressed (b) impressed the judges.

Cesar: You impress me, TJ. You're (a) somebody else (b) something else on that board!

TJ: Ah, come on, (a) stop it (b) give it up, will you?

Cesar: But I've seen you fly on a skateboard. It's (a) astounding (b) amazing.

TJ: Yeah, well, things (a) have been pretty good (b) have been going good. You'll never (a) believe (b) understand what the latest is.

Cesar: What?

TJ: Nike wants me to (a) shoot (b) do a commercial. They've been calling my agent.

Cesar: Wow! I don't (a) get it (b) believe that.

TJ: (a) You best (b) You'd better believe it, my friend. I'm going to get (a) top dollar (b) some big bucks for doing it, too.

Cesar: You're (a) getting famous (b) going big time now. I can't believe I even know you.

TJ: Great, huh? I'm going to be on TV!

Cesar: Yeah! Pretty soon you're not (a) going to remember (b) going to have time for someone like me.

TJ: No way, Cesar. You know (a) my friends are (b) my career is important.

Cesar: Yeah, but now you're hitting (a) the big money (b) the big time. Everything's (a) going to change (b) going to stop.

TJ: You know I'm (a) just one of the boys (b) just a regular guy.

Cesar: No, you're not.

TJ: Yes, I am. I've got parents and (a) a beautiful sister (b) a bratty sister, just like you. I (a) took piano lessons (b) played baseball when I was little, and I (a) stay at home (b) go to church on Sundays. I like (a) watching television (b) watching cartoons, and my mom makes me (a) clean up my room (b) take out the trash. And I worry about (a) having too many friends (b) not having a girlfriend. See? I'm just·like (a) everybody else (b) nobody else.

Cesar: I don't think so. Nobody else I know is doing a Nike commercial. You've (a) made it big (b) got it made, TJ.

TJ: Yeah, but the problem is (a) my teachers (b) my parents.

Cesar: What's up?

TJ: To really make it big, I've got to (a) be a professional (b) go on the pro tour, and the only way I can go pro is to (a) stay away from (b) drop out of school, but they (a) prefer I don't (b) don't want me to. They say I'm (a) running (b) ruining my future. But I may not get another chance — two years from now may (a) be too late (b) be all right.

Cesar: So (a) what do you think you'll do (b) what're you going to do?

TJ: I've got to (a) give it up (b) go for it. I'm at the (a) top of my game (b) peak of my skills right now, and that's what counts.

Cesar: Yeah, you've got to do what (a) you've got to do (b) you want to do

BONUS QUESTION

TJ wants to drop out of school, but his parents disagree.
Write a conversation between TJ and his parents.

Real World Listening

Listen to the conversation. Fill in the missing parts.

always brings me	had just eaten dinner	kissed me	not only her	such a flirt
appreciative	have it much worse	leans out the door	rent my apartment	the older couple
been coming up	it's kind of weird	like I'm 17	remind him	when I got home
gave me a hug	it was cute	nice to feel	sits and watches me	wouldn't leave

Kara: Steve, remember _____ that I _____ from?

Steve: Yeah?

Kara: Well, the woman has _____ to see how I'm doing. At first I was really _____, you know, it's _____ that people are concerned when you live alone.

Steve: Yeah, it is nice.

Kara: Now, though, she comes every day... sometimes more than once! She _____ homemade soup...

Steve: Homemade soup! That is so great! I wish someone cooked for me.

Kara: Sure, having some home-cooked food is a treat, but she _____ to make sure I eat it! Last time, I _____ when she came over and insisted that I finish a whole bowl. She _____ until I did!

Steve: Oh, come one, you could _____ .

Kara: And, every time I go out she _____ to ask where I'm going . It's _____ again!

Steve: Would you rather have loud neighbors who kept you up all night?

Kara: Well, it's _____ . It's the old man, too. He's _____ , and I've always thought _____ You know, an old man, 80 years old, still flirting.

Steve: Uh huh...

Kara: So, today _____ , he came up to me, _____ ...

Steve: Yeah, so what...?

Kara: And then, he _____ on the cheek...!

Steve: Oh no. Well, maybe you _____ of his granddaughter.

Kara: Well, yeah, but don't you think _____ for him to kiss me ?

BONUS QUESTION

Imagine you are Kara. Write a letter to an advice column asking for advice. Then write a lett‹ in response to Kara.

Real World Listening

Listen to the conversation. Choose the correct words.

Rachel: So, Susie, how was the plane ride from (a) New York (b) London?

Susie: Oh, I don't know. (a) What I was thinking about (b) All I could think about was getting here and (a) going shopping (b) doing some shopping.

Rachel: Hmmm.

Susie: Rachel, (a) what's the matter (b) what's wrong?

Rachel: Susie, I thought you came (a) to visit me (b) to see me! Isn't that (a) more important (b) more worth while than shopping?

Susie: Oh come on, Rachel. Shopping is (a) so much fun (b) so bonding!

Rachel: All right, I'll take you (a) to the shops (b) to the stores. What are you (a) looking for (b) planning to buy?

Susie: Well, I want a (a) purse (b) handbag from Prada, and maybe one of their (a) black leather dresses (b) black satin dresses ...

Rachel: Oh no...

Susie: ... a couple of (a) shirts (b) skirts from Donna Karan, you know, the ones that are really (a) tight (b) fitted, a pair of jeans ...

Rachel: (a) Whoa! (b) Wait a minute! How much money (a) do you have (b) did you bring, anyway?

Susie: Oh Rachel, you know (a) I save up (b) I prepare to come to New York every year to go shopping. Now that you're (a) living (b) studying here, I want to go with you. So what are you going to get?

Rachel: Are you (a) joking (b) kidding, Susie? I've got two words for you - (a) "no money" (b) "student budget." I can't afford to (a) buy any clothing (b) spend money on clothes!

Susie: Well, you're just (a) a neat and clean person (b) a jeans and T-shirt person, aren't you? I am going to (a) have a good time (b) enjoy myself no matter how much (a) I spend (b) it costs. I'm (a) on holiday (b) on vacation. Look, Rachel, I'll (a) get something for you (b) buy you something, a new blouse, or skirt, (a) anything you want (b) whatever you want.

Rachel: Well, I don't want anyone to buy me something (a) I don't really want (b) I can't afford myself.

Susie: Oh, don't worry about that. And, there is no need to (a) thank me (b) spank me. It's (a) the least I can do (b) the most I can do since you'll be (a) cooking dinner (b) putting me up every night while I'm here.

Rachel: Dinner? (a) What do you mean? (b) What are you talking about?

BONUS QUESTION

Some people say that "clothes define the person." What do you think?
Write your opinion.

Real World Listening

🔘 **Listen to the conversation. Fill in the missing parts.**

Did he know	management	the job interview	worked in travel management
expects the manager to be	perfect for that job	the management position	what I thought
got the job	showed him	told him	Why did I bother
got a degree	so it's not because	understand	
hired me	supervise	what he said	
I got the management job	the person they hired	what they want	

Richard: Hello?

Irma: Hi, it's me.

Richard: Oh, hi! How was _____ ?

Irma: Well, he _____ .

Richard: You _____ ? The _____ job? Oh, that's great!

Irma: No, I didn't say _____ . He hired me for a job in customer service, selling tours to Asia.

Richard: Just customer service? But what about _____ ? You were _____ . You can _____ people. You _____ the business.

Irma: I know. I _____ my resume. I _____ that I _____ for five years back home, and that I even _____ in Business Management here in the U.S.

Richard: Oh, I can't believe that. You're perfectly qualified for that management position.

Irma: That's _____ . It's not fair! _____ going to college here.

Richard: Wait a minute. _____ that you were applying for the management position?

Irma: Of course. And you know _____ ?

Richard: What?

Irma: He said that everyone really _____ someone from the local community. But _____ is from New York. And she's a woman, too, _____ I am a woman. So that means the problem is my English.

Richard: But your English is fantastic!

Irma: But I'm not a native speaker, and I guess that's _____ for __ management job.

Richard: Well, you know, you spend a little time at the customer service job and you can work your w__ up to the management position.

BONUS QUESTION
What do you think about Irma's situation? Write your opinion.

Real World Listening

Listen to the conversation. Correct the errors in the script.

Amy: I know I have a photograph of Thomas around here somewhere. Oh, here's one.

Mika: Wow! He's so strange! He looks like a Roman statue.

Amy: Yeah, he is very interesting. But that's not what I thought when I first saw him.

Mika: Didn't you?

Amy: No. You know what I was impressed by when I first met him? He has a really thick beard.

Mika: What?

Amy: Yeah. His face was just really hairy. Plus, his clothes were way more shabby than I generally like. He just wasn't my kind of person. And in addition to all of that, he was taller than me.

Mika: So how come you started dating him?

Amy: Well, he was just really sensitive and funny and it was so much fun just hanging out with him. And the second time we went out he just blew me away with his sense of humor.

Mika: Really, how so?

Amy: He was just really fun to be with.

Mika: But still, if all those things were weird, about his hands and all...

Amy: Well, you know, none of that mattered once I got to know him better. His personality and how we got along just made it clear to me that he's the one for me.

Mika: So, when's the engagement?

BONUS QUESTION

Think about someone you like. What "good" qualities do you like? What "bad" qualities do you overlook, or not notice any more?

Real World Listening

Listen to the conversation. Put the lines in order.

Eddie: ___ Heard what?

Marty: ___ Yeah, you're right. But now everything in this house is going to be Kristy and Shawna, Kristy and Shawna. Or else Grandma.

Eddie: ___ Ah, come on, Marty. They aren't brats.

Eddie: ___ I don't think that will change. You know your mom wants to take care of everybody. She doesn't want to say no if anybody needs her.

Marty: ___ Kristy and Shawna are moving in with us.

Eddie: ___ Yeah, I heard. Simon got transferred to Florida, right?

Eddie: ___ Yeah, sometimes I do, too.

Marty: ___ I wish we were back in our old house — just us, Mom and Dad.

Eddie: ___ Hey, what's up with you, Marty? You look kind of bummed out.

Marty: ___ And I wish Mom and Dad wouldn't try to solve everybody's problems.

Eddie: ___ Yeah, there's a lot of us now, that's for sure. I hear we're going to have to sleep in the liv room so that Kristy and Shawna can have our room.

Marty: ___ But nobody ever asks me what I want!

Eddie: ___ Hey, don't get mad at your grandma. She's in a lot of pain, you know.

Marty: ___ You haven't heard?

Eddie: ___ Hey, maybe I can help you with your homework. Bring it here.

Marty: ___ Really? You mean it? I'm really stuck on this math.

Eddie: ___ Kids never get to say what goes on in their house. That's the way it is.

Marty: ___ Yeah, but you know what it's going to mean? Mom and Dad aren't going to have any tir for us anymore. And it's going to get even more crowded here. Just one big happy family

Marty: ___ Yeah, so he and Lily got to go there first and do a whole bunch of stuff. That means tha we get stuck with the twin brats.

Marty: ___ I know. I'm not really mad at her. I'm mad at Mom and Dad. They used to always have time to help me with my homework, or play games with me, but they're always too busy And now it's going to get even worse.

Eddie: ___ Sure. While things are kind of tough aound here, I'll help you out as much as I can.

BONUS QUESTION

Eddie and Marty have to make some "accommodations" to get along in their family. What some accommodations that people in your family have to make?

Real World Listening

Listen to the conversation. Fill in the missing parts.

onderful place to live
being wrapped
't take it
n't you know
ling it
w long have you been living
w to be more efficient
nd of like it

it's better this way
putting those bags
taping that bag shut
that's the way it is
time to sit down
to do whatever you want
to your way of doing things
to stick them in a napkin

You're not going to last
while I'm walking
Why don't you just relax
When I was in the U.S.
what they do
what are you talking about
wrapping each pastry

ve: I can't believe these people. I can't believe _____ .

sh: Calm down, Steve, _____ ? What is it this time?

ve: Look at this. I just bought a donut. I'm so sick of the clerk _____ individually, then taping the bags shut, then _____ in another bag, _____ down, and then _____ .
    I _____ anymore. It's crazy and it's bad for the environment.

sh: _____ here? Don't you know _____ ?

ve: I just want them _____ for me, so I can eat _____ to class.

sh: There you go again. _____ it's rude to eat while you walk?

ve: I'm so tired of this place. I don't have _____ and eat.
    People here are too inflexible, and they have too many rules.

sh: Yeah, right, Steve, so you're going to convert everybody here _____ ?

ve: Yeah! There has to be more individual freedom _____ .

sh: _____ and go with the flow?

ve: Go with the flow? The whole system is a waste of my time. The clerks here should learn _____ like in the U.S.

sh: What are you talking about? _____ , the clerks were really rude. They just ignore you, and seem offended if you want anything. Don't you think _____ ?

ve: Are you kidding?

sh: Well, _____ . It's nice to relax and enjoy the moment while your packages _____ . I like all of the traditions, and the care and attention that people give you, and the manners. To me, it's _____ .

ve: I think you're nuts.

sh: _____ long, mate.

NUS QUESTION

at is one thing in your culture that visitors have trouble understanding? Why?
w do they react?

81

Real World Listening

Listen to the conversation. Choose the correct words.

Andy: Hey, Bob. How are you? Come and see what (a) **I have** (b) **I've got**.

Bob: Is that (a) **a** (b) **another** new computer?

Andy: Yeah. Look how (a) **cool** (b) **fast** it is.

Bob: Wow! I (a) **don't believe you** (b) **can't believe it**. And I thought your (a) **old** (b) **other** computer was fast!

Andy: It is fast, but this one's like (a) **light** (b) **lightning**.

Bob: And the picture's so (a) **clear** (b) **bright**.

Andy: Mmm. Isn't it? The color is pretty (a) **impressed** (b) **impressive**, too, don't you think?

Bob: Yeah. You always have the (a) **best** (b) **latest**, don't you?

Andy: You bet. This machine is right on (a) **the leading edge** (b) **the cutting edge** of technology. You wouldn't believe how much it can do. (a) **Apart from** (b) **In addition to** e-mail and free Internet service, I can watch (a) **videos** (b) **TV** on it while surfing. With this new desktop (a) **program** (b) **software**, I can watch TV, e-mail, streamline videos, and scan artwork. And it's not that (a) **expensive** (b) **inexpensive** to upgrade, either. Ah, speaking of computers, how's (a) **yours** (b) **your computer**? Still (a) **like it** (b) **happy with it**?

Bob: Yeah, it's fine. Thanks!

Andy: I know I gave you (a) **a bargain** (b) **a good deal**. It was only a year old. Still, are you sure it (a) **is what you need** (b) **meets all your needs**? Maybe you should think about (a) **expanding** (b) **upgrading**.

Bob: You know me — the only things I (a) **use** (b) **need** a computer for are e-mail and word processing.

Andy: Yeah, but does it give you room to (a) **extend** (b) **expand**? If you want to be able to do more two years from now, will your computer be able to (a) **manage** (b) **handle** it?

Bob: Well, I don't know. But I kind of doubt that I'll need a new one anytime soon.

Andy: Yeah, but with computers, there's always a new model (a) **appearing** (b) **coming out** that can do so much more. If you don't (a) **stay ahead of** (b) **keep up with** technology, you'll (a) **be unprepared** (b) **get left behind**.

Bob: Well, what's (a) **so bad about that** (b) **wrong with that**?

BONUS QUESTION
How has technology changed your life? How do you think it will change your life in the future?

Real World Listening

Listen to the conversation. Fill in the missing parts.

a glass of wine	have a baby	kidding me	pregnant	the last thing you need
a number of things	How are you	might find exciting	regular exercise	was supposed to be
been a little tired	I'm stressed out	need a cigarette	stop drinking alcohol	wake me up
emphasize enough	I'm afraid you have to	not an alcoholic	surprise me	while you're pregnant
give up everything	it is amazing	only one of them	take this seriously	What else is there
have birth defects	kind of upset	on top of all that	the only way	

Doctor: Hi, Julie. _____ ?

Julie: Hey, Dr. Cassidy. I'm actually fine. It's just that I've _____
the last few days, and my stomach's _____ .

Doctor: Well, that doesn't _____ . I have some news that you
_____ . You're _____ .

Julie: No way!

Doctor: Yes, you're going to _____ .

Julie: Are you _____ ? Ah, I _____ .

Doctor: That's _____ . You need to stop smoking,
and immediately.

Julie: But I can't stop smoking.

Doctor: For your baby's health, Julie, _____ .

Julie: But smoking is _____ I can relax! It helps me when
_____ .

Doctor: Now, there are _____ that are extremely important for
pregnant mothers, and not smoking is _____ . Another is
to _____ . Do you drink?

Julie: Well, I have _____ with dinner, but I'm
_____ . And I thought a little bit
good for you anyway.

Doctor: If you drink _____ , your child could
_____ . I cannot _____ ,
Julie, the importance of quitting.

Julie: OK, then. _____ ?

Doctor: Well, coffee.

Julie: Do I have to _____ I enjoy? I need coffee to
_____ in the morning.

Doctor: I'm afraid, Julie, you'll have to stop drinking that, too. Caffeine affects the baby's heart rate. And
it's also important to get in _____ .

Julie: You're kidding! I have to quit smoking, stop drinking alcohol and coffee, and
_____ , I have to start exercising? Boy,
_____ anybody ever gets pregnant.

Doctor: I really hope you'll _____ , Julie.

BONUS QUESTION

Imagine you are Julie's doctor. What advice would you give to Julie about her habits?

Real World Listening

Listen to the conversation. Fill in the missing parts.

a ketchup bottle	had reservations	squirted ketchup	threw the bottle
a sweet little Thai woman	I started arguing	stranded	to get really angry
apologize to her	paid for our tickets	such a fool	What happened
be more patient	pulled up	That wasn't	we'd been cheated
ended up	pulled up	that's not	were traveling
felt so stupid	shrugged	the bus didn't come	you have
get us a taxi	snapped	the last straw	
got to do with	sort of	the van drove away	

Sue: Randy, What's going on in this picture? It looks like _____ blood all over your shirt.

Randy: No, _____ blood. It's ketchup.

Sue: Ketchup? _____?

Randy: This happened when Tim and I _____ around Asia. We were in Bangkok.

Sue: Yeah...

Randy: And we _____ to catch an overnight bus to Chiang Mai.

Sue: Yeah.

Randy: And we were waiting at a kind of restaurant that was _____ a travel agency...and we went early, but _____, and I was getting kind of worried...

Sue: Yeah, but what's that _____ ketchup?

Randy: So, I was beginning to wonder if _____, because we'd already _____ in advance...

Sue: Right...

Randy: Then, finally, a van _____, and we thought, no, this is not the bus...but then everyone else who was waiting pushed right past us and jumped in, and, bam!, just like that, _____. And then, _____ who was the travel agent who sold us the tickets, came up to us.

Sue: Yeah, and...

Randy: And she said,"Why you no get on?" And Tim was like, "_____ the bus, was it?" "Only one. Why you not get on?" And I didn't know what she was talking about.

Sue: So what happened?

Randy: Well, the travel agent just _____

and turned and went inside her shop. Neither of us could believe it. I started _____, like we'd been cheated. Now it's dark, we're _____ in this little restaurant...

Sue: Oh, no...

Randy: I followed her inside. _____. I told her, "We paid for the bus. You didn't tell us to look for a van. Now you have to _____ to Chiang Mai. Now." I started pointing at the clock. I think that was _____ for the woman, because she started shouting, "You no go. You no go Chiang Mai!" She grabbed _____ off the table, you know, one of those plastic squirt ketchup bottles, and she _____ at me!

Sue: No! She didn't!

Randy: Yeah! She did. And then she _____ at me. And Tim _____ the picture. Just then the same van _____ and the woman said, "Now you go."

Sue: So you got on the van.

Randy: Yeah. We _____ at the bus terminal, where this big, air-conditioned tour bus was waiting to go to Chiang Mai. And all the people who had pushed ahead of us earlier were there, waiting to leave. I _____ for getting angry at the woman and making _____ of myself.

Sue: You must have felt terrible.

Randy: Yeah, I wished there was some way I could go back and _____. I realized that I have to _____ especially when I'm in another country.

BONUS QUESTION

Do you know a "travel story" like this? Write the travel story in a conversation form.

Real World Listening

Listen to the commercial. Choose the correct words.

Ed: Are you **(a) worried (b) concerned** about having enough money? Are you worried about **(a) making ends meet (b) paying your bills**? Well, **(a) don't worry anymore (b) worry no more**!

Customer -1: I used to **(a) watch (b) take care of** every penny. But now **(a) I'm worth (b) I have assets of** four million dollars, and it's all **(a) due to (b) thanks to** Steven Crowe!

Customer -2: I used to get **(a) heartaches (b) headaches** from worrying about money. I had a lot of credit card **(a) bills (b) debt**, and my mortgage **(a) bills (b) payments** were killing me. Then I got Steven Crowe's **(a) programs (b) videos**, and learned how to **(a) earn (b) make** real money.

Ed: "Real money." That's the name of this 3- **(a) CD (b) video** set by Steven Crowe. Let Steven **(a) show (b) teach** you how to become **(a) personally (b) financially** independent buying and selling real estate.

Steven: Hi! I'm Steven Crowe. I used to **(a) worry (b) be worried** about money, too. I felt like a **(a) hero (b) victim** of the system. But then I found a way to make the **(a) system (b) market** work — for me.

Ed: What's the **(a) idea (b) trick**, Steven?

Steven: There's no trick, Ed. It's **(a) easy (b) simple**, once you **(a) understand (b) comprehend** how real estate really works. All you need to know is how to **(a) acquire (b) buy** low and sell high. And that's **(a) exactly (b) precisely** what my videos **(a) instruct (b) teach** you to do.

Ed: And you can **(a) get (b) become** really rich?

Steven: Just **(a) ask (b) listen** to some people who have "Real Money."

Customer-1: After I got the "Real Money" videos, I bought my first **(a) house (b) business**, following Steven's simple **(a) ideas (b) rules**. Six months later I sold it and bought two more houses. A year after that, I had **(a) plenty of (b) enough** money to **(a) quit my job (b) start my business**. Now I have more money than I'll ever need, and it's such a **(a) great (b) wonderful** feeling.

Steven: I want you to have that feeling, too. And you **(a) can (b) will**.

Ed: Call now to order "Real Money." **(a) 1-800-289-7325 (b) 1-800-298-7235**. That's 1-800-BUY-REAL. Only three **(a) amounts (b) payments** of **(a) 19.95 (b) 29.95** each, plus shipping and handling. All major credit cards welcome. Get it today, for a worry-free tomorrow! Results may vary.

BONUS QUESTION

Think of a "get-rich-quick" product or scheme. Write an advertisement for it.

Real World Listening

🔊 **Listen to the conversation. Fill in the missing parts.**

a bigger place	concrete and steel	late	more worthwhile	tired already
an hour and a half	do it all over	like a sardine	move closer	time to enjoy it
be nice	even started	love living	my whole life	walk here
bring a book	feel like	long	read the newspaper	wake up
closer to the city	five days a week	look at the trees	so many people	
complaining	get really crowded	make it	so fresh and clean	
commute	good idea	missed my connection	stupid train	

Lori: Oh, good, you're here. Another bad _____ today?

Carrie: Yeah, sorry, I'm _____. The _____ was late again, and I _____, and... gosh, I'm _____, and the day hasn't _____.

Lori: How _____ is your commute?

Carrie: Almost _____, on a good day. Three hours of my life every day, _____, you know? I've got to _____ at six in the morning just to _____ in to work by nine or so. I _____ a techno-serf.

Lori: That is long. I can _____ in 15 minutes. But you know, at least your commute is green. You can _____ and small towns. It must _____.

Carrie: For the first 20 minutes, yeah. But as soon as the train gets _____, it's all _____. That's when it starts to _____. Today _____ were in the train that I felt _____ in a big sardine can.

Lori: Well, you could always _____ to the office.

Carrie: But I _____ in the country. The air is _____ and I can have _____, and it's safe and all that... I just wish I had more _____. Sometimes it seems like _____ is: get up early, take the train, work all day, take the train home, go to bed, — and then wake up and _____ again.

Lori: Well, can't you find a way to make the trip _____?

Carrie: Well, I _____ and sometimes I _____, but I don't really enjoy it.

Lori: How about audio tapes or CDs? There's novels or language learning tapes, relaxation tapes, all kinds of stuff on tape and CD.

Carrie: Yeah, _____, maybe I'll look into it. Anything'll be better than _____ about this commute all the time.

Lori: Yeah, that's for sure!

BONUS QUESTION
How do you spend your "free time" during a typical day? What else could you do? Write about

Real World Listening

Listen to the conversation. Fill in the missing parts.

burst into tears
climbed out of bed
could hear people
  talking
come out the window
crawled out
had a chance
happened to you

helped us
hugged each other
I shouted
lasted 24 seconds
must have been
  horrifying
near as strong
Not any more

pulled the covers
rolling like waves
scariest thing
stopped
this horrible sound
totally flattened
to figure out
tried to go out

someone shouted
Surviving
was bouncing
was jammed
was living
were still asleep
were living

were down on the
  ground
What did you do
what happened
What'd you guys do
who lived on the
  first floor
won't open

Anna: Margaret, what's the _____ that ever _____ ?

Margaret: The scariest thing? _____ the San Jose earthquake.

Anna: You were in the San Jose earthquake? Tell me _____ .

Margaret: Well, I _____ in an apartment downtown with my friend, Julia. And we _____ on a Tuesday morning, and a little after six o'clock, there was _____ ... and the floor _____ and _____ , all, like, at the same time.

Anna: My gosh! _____ ?

Margaret: It took a second or two _____ that it was an earthquake. Then I _____ and under the table, and _____ at Julia to come, but she just _____ over her head like it was a bad dream or something.

Anna: Whoa!

Margaret: It _____ , and then it _____ . And Julia and I _____ outside, so we _____ the front door, but it _____ shut. And then the first aftershock hit.

Anna: That _____ !

Margaret: Oh, it was. Nowhere _____ but it was still scary. We just _____ and kept saying, "What do we do?"

Anna: _____ ?

Margaret: Well, I remember _____ , "Get out of there, quickly!" And we shouted back, "We can't! The door _____ ." So they said, "Well, _____ ." But I called out, "It's too high up," because we _____ on the second floor. "_____ ," the person shouted back. So we looked out the window and, sure enough, we _____ !

Anna: Your second-floor apartment was on the ground?!

Margaret: We couldn't believe it. We opened the window and _____ , and somebody _____ over all this rubble. And once we were down safely, we turned around and looked back at our apartment building. The whole first floor was gone — it was just _____ . And then Julia looked at me and said, "Margaret. Mr. Sanchez!" He was this elderly man _____ .

Anna: Oh, no. How horrible!

Margaret: Yeah. Julia and I both just _____ . He never _____ .

‍BONUS QUESTION

‍Interview someone who has been in a disaster like this one. **What happened? Write their story.**

Real World Listening

Listen to the program. Fill in the missing parts.

a Korean family	in love with	they're trying to understand
about your problem	like to see you	told my parents
afraid of telling them	Marry the person	to be divided
always expected me	married a Chinese man	to marry him
came to see us	never came to visit us	very angry
Don't give in	our little girl was born	very traditional
don't wait four years	the part of the show	very traditional
go against	they disowned me	won't let me

Dr. Monroe: This is Dr. Ellen Monroe on Love Talk. This is _____ where we listen to our callers' advice. Tonight we have Sunhee, a woman with a love problem. Sunhee, tell us _____.

Sunhee: I'm from _____, and I'm _____ a man from India that I met here in the U.S.

Dr. Monroe: Okay, and...

Sunhee: He's asked me _____, and I said yes.

Dr. Monroe: So what is the problem?

Sunhee: It's my parents — they're _____ — so I'm _____ that I'm engaged. I'm worried that they _____ marry him.

Dr. Monroe: Hmm...

Sunhee: I can't _____ my parents' will. But this is the man I want to marry.

Dr. Monroe: Hmm. That's Sunhee's problem, folks. Now, what's your advice to her?

Dr. Monroe: Hello. What's your advice for our worried friend?

Carla: Hello. I'm Carla, from Canada, and I _____ five years ago. When I first _____ I wanted to marry a foreigner with different religious beliefs, they were _____ — You see, they're _____ — they've _____ to marry someone Canadian, from the same religious background.

Dr. Monroe: Then what happened?

Carla: For four years, they hardly talked to me and they _____. It was like _____ ...

Dr. Monroe: Four years, you say. After four years something changed?

Carla: Yes. When _____, I sent my parents a picture of her, and wrote "Your granddaughter would _____." A week later they called and a month after that they _____ — well, they came to see my daughter, anyway. Now they're trying — they still aren't comfortable with my husband but _____ him.

Dr. Monroe: So, what's your advice?

Carla: _____ to tradition. _____ you love. But have your first child soon — _____ like I did. That's too long _____ from your parents.

Dr. Monroe: Sounds like good advice to me.

BONUS QUESTION

What is your opinion about international marriages? What are the advantages and disadvantage

Real World Listening

Listen to the conversation. Put the lines in order.

Richard: ___ What for? What's wrong with it the way it is?

Sarah: ___ At this rate, we're never going to find anything we both like.

Richard: ___ College is about having parties. About having friends over. I don't want something that looks like my parents' house.

Sarah: ___ Are you kidding? It's so empty.

Richard: ___ Homey? Okay, I'm not looking for homey. I'm a college student.

Sarah: ___ It doesn't have to cost a lot.

Richard: ___ Yeah, well, at least we can agree on that.

Sarah: ___ Parties, Richard? Richard, we are not going to have any time to party. We are going to be way too busy studying. That's what we're in college for!

Richard: ___ A few things? Oh, man, this is going to cost money.

Sarah: ___ Look. It doesn't have to look like your parents' house. We just need a few simple things like chairs. Maybe some plants. You know, it'll just make it nice and homey.

Richard: ___ Hey, that's a good idea. We could get a couple of psychedelic posters and a lava lamp. Get a black light. Crank up the stereo. We could have cool parties here.

Sarah: ___ But, Richard, we're not the only ones that are going to be here. We want to have friends over, you know, have people over to study. They've got to have places to sit.

Richard: ___ Why can't we just leave it the way it is? I like it. I feel comfortable here. You start putting a lot of nice things around and it's going to be a museum.

Sarah: ___ You know, Richard, I really think we ought to fix up our apartment a little.

Richard: ___ Come on. A room is just a room. Why do we have to fill it up with a bunch of junk? Besides, it costs money.

Sarah: ___ Well, it doesn't have to be that expensive. I know this really neat little thrift store around the corner. We can go there and get a few simple things, just make it feel like a home.

BONUS QUESTION
How would you like to fix up your room, apartment, or house?

Real World Listening

🎧 **Listen to the conversation. Fill in the missing parts.**

can't hide things	have a lot of memories	passed away
dealing with loss	have some wonderful memories	share his story
don't lose those memories	how you're managing	share so many years
expected her to go	just wanted it to be over	telling us how
get to know someone	losing a spouse	tried to keep up
had a lot of good times	must have been very difficult	when we lose someone
had it for about a year	no one can fill up	

Whitney: Welcome to Life's Concerns. I'm your host, Whitney Opal. Today our program is about _____. One of the hardest things in life is _____ after so many years together. Mr. Clayton Hayes is here today to _____. Thank you for joining us, Mr. Hayes.

Clayton: Call me Clayton, please.

Whitney: Okay, Clayton, I'd like to ask you a few questions about _____. Is that okay?

Clayton: Yes, that's fine. I can talk about it.

Whitney: All right. Well, your wife _____ two years ago — is that correct?

Clayton: Yep. Maggie was 79, just about to turn 80 when she passed away. I never really _____. She was still too young.

Whitney: I'm sorry. Do you mind _____ she died?

Clayton: Cancer. She _____, but it seemed longer than that to me. And she was in so much pain at the end. Oh.

Whitney: I'm really sorry. That _____ for you.

Clayton: Yeah. At the end there, you could tell she _____. She _____ a cheerful face for me, but you _____ from someone you've been married to for 56 years, you know.

Whitney: I'm sure that's true. You _____ pretty well in 56 years, don't you?

Clayton: Oh, you bet you do. You _____ of your life with someone, and when they're gone, oh, there's a big hole that _____. You just feel lonely. Very, very lonely.

Whitney: I imagine you _____, as well.

Clayton: Oh, yeah. We _____, Maggie and me. Boy, the stories I could tell! ...

Whitney: Well, Clayton, you sure do _____ from your time with Maggie to celebrate!

Clayton: Yeah, I sure do.

Whitney: I think it's important to remember that _____ close to us, we _____. The person is still with us in that way.

BONUS QUESTION

Tell about someone who died who had been close to you. What good memories do you have of that person?

90

Real World Listening

Listen to the conversation. Fill in the missing parts.

any problems there may have been	I'm a liar	treat a valued customer
being treated like that	let me speak to the manager	was treated so rudely
exchange this shirt	planning to exchange this shirt	wants to talk to you
exchange this item	see your receipt	want my money back
How can I help you	take responsibility for her behavior	when I bought it
How can I be of assistance	thanks for understanding	
I'll just exchange it	there's a stain, all right	

Customer: Excuse me, ma'am.

Clerk: Yeah? _____ ?

Customer: I'd like to _____ . It has a flaw... it's stained right over here.

Clerk: Let me see ... Yep, _____ . How'd that happen?

Customer: It was there _____ .

Clerk: Mmm, don't think so.

Customer: Uhh, it's true.

Clerk: We check every item. I don't think so.

Customer: You saying _____ ?

Clerk: No, but we're careful, I mean, it's our job.

Customer: OK, look, just _____ .

Clerk: OK, I'm sorry. What was it that you wanted again? To exchange it, or — ?

Customer: I want to speak to the manager.

Clerk: Fine. Whatever. Dee! A customer _____ .

Manager: _____ ?

Customer: Well, I came in _____ — and it has a stain, see —

Manager: Yes...

Customer: But I _____ by this person, I just _____ . I'm not shopping here anymore.

Manager: Well, I'm very sorry about _____ . Can you tell me what happened here?

Customer: She accused me of staining this shirt.

Clerk: Hey, I was just trying to make sure...

Manager: Why don't you go to my office and wait for me... Look, I'm very sorry. I _____ . But we'd really like to keep you as a customer. And I'd be glad to _____ for you, or give you a full refund, whichever you'd like.

Customer: I don't know. I don't like _____ . I don't think she cares.

Manager: Rest assured she will be taught how to _____ .

Customer: Well, OK, I guess _____ . I like the shirt, after all.

Manager: Oh, wonderful. Well, _____ . Now, may I _____ , please?

BONUS QUESTION:

Describe a situation in which you received very unusual service. Write a dialogue.

Real World Listening

Listen to the conversation. Correct the errors in the script.

Rob: Hey, Tony! What's up?

Tony: Hey, Rob. Check this out. I got a package from my dad.

Rob: Oh, yes! Money, I hope.

Tony: Nah. It's a comic book. Twenty-Minute Meals. It's perfect for us, don't you think?

Rob: Yeah, I guess. But I wish she would've sent you food instead.

Tony: Think about it, though. No more instant ramen, no more pizza. Twenty minutes in the kitchen, and voila! we have a well-balanced dinner. Are you with me?

Rob: Whatever you say, Chef Tony. Let's look at it. How about this? Super Nachos. Now that's my kind of meal.

Tony: All right! Let's go. What ingredients do we need?

Rob: What we really need is for you to find someone who can cook.

Tony: Yeah, right. And then you'll find one, too, and they can take turns cooking for us. So what are the ingredients?

Rob: Chips, salsa, a can of chili, and shredded wheat. That sounds pretty difficult.

Tony: Well, we've got a full bag of nacho chips. Think that's enough?

Rob: It'll have to be. Let's see what's in the refrigerator . . . We've got lots of soda..... half a meatball sandwich... Cheese! We've got that. Ooh, it's kind of old, though.

Tony: Kind of? It's blue! Do we have any chili?

Rob: Sorry, man, I think I ate it last night.

Tony: That wasn't yours. Anyway, I had a couple of jars. There must be at least one left.

Rob: Let's see... A box of cereal... some instant ramen... and a jar of peanut butter. That's it.

Tony: Oh, darn. It looks like we can't make nachos tonight after all.

Rob: I guess we can't. Well, what are we going to do? Instant ramen for the third night in a row? With peanut butter?

Tony: I'm so sick of that stuff! Let's go to the supermarket and get what we need to make Super Nachos.

Rob: Yeah, and on the way, let's stop for hamburgers or a pizza.

Tony: Yeah, good idea...

BONUS QUESTION
Think of one food you know how to make. Write a recipe for it.

Real World Listening

Listen to the conversation. Fill in the missing parts.

at it again	fighting with each other	in other countries' business	resolve this problem
care so much	get along together	keep talking about	start playing with
disagree	get involved	kind of scary	Their usual role
don't care	have more power	Isn't that serious	threatening each other
fighting	hear in the news	problems of its own	trying to intimidate

David: What's this I _____ about India and Pakistan?

Nehal: They're _____ .

David: What do you mean — they're at it again?

Nehal: They just cannot _____ .

David: This news story says they're testing missiles. _____ ?

Nehal: Well, it's more like flexing their muscles than actually doing something serious. They're just _____ each other.

David: It's _____ , though, isn't it?

Nehal: I'm used to it by now. They've been _____ my whole life.

David: But why?

Nehal: They've been _____ about Kashmir. They _____ about who controls Kashmir.

David: Yeah? What is it that's so important about Kashmir anyway? I mean, why? Why do India and Pakistan _____ about Kashmir?

Nehal: Actually, they _____ about Kashmir.

David: Huh? What do you mean?

Nehal: No. All India and Pakistan care about is _____ . Each one wants to _____ than the other.

David: So why do they _____ Kashmir?

Nehal: It's just an excuse.

David: Still, I don't like it when they _____ nuclear weapons. Maybe the U.N. should _____ .

Nehal: Ah, yes. _____ as the great peacekeeper.

David: Don't you think the U.N. could _____ ?

Nehal: I don't think so. The U.N. doesn't need to get involved _____ It has enough _____ .

BONUS QUESTION
What is a serious problem in the world today? What is causing it? How can it be resolved?

Notes

Notes

Welcome to the *Impact* Series

■ Coursebooks

■ Conversation courses

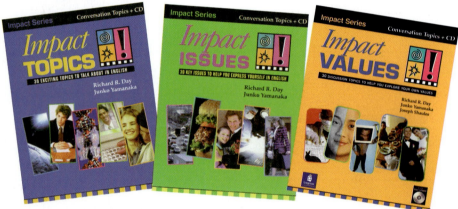

■ Skills courses

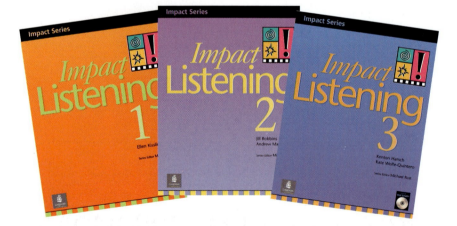

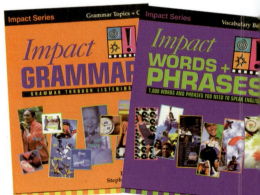

Visit our website for more ideas and teacher discussion.
www.impactseries.com